PEOPLE OF THE JAGUAR

Jaguar attacking Indian woodcutter on the coast of Surinam, north-east South America. Note the human-like stance and build of the jaguar. From *Amerikaansche Voyagien*, A. Van Berkel, 1695. *Photo, Courtesy of the Bodleian Library, Oxford* Ref. 4°A.97.Th.BS.FRTSP1.

PEOPLE OF THE JAGUAR

The Living Spirit
of Ancient America

Nicholas J. Saunders

SOUVENIR PRESS

First published 1989 by Souvenir Press Ltd,
43 Great Russell Street, London WC1B 3PA
and simultaneously in Canada

ISBN 0 285 62892 5

Photoset in Great Britain by
Rowland Phototypesetting Ltd,
Bury St Edmunds, Suffolk
Printed and bound in Great Britain by
WBC Ltd, Bristol and Maesteg

For Roxanne,
'Little Star'

ACKNOWLEDGEMENTS

This book is the result of sixteen years' interest in both the archaeology and anthropology of Central and South America, and in particular, the fascination which the prehistoric inhabitants displayed towards the image of the jaguar, America's largest cat; a fascination which has survived to the verge of the twenty-first century.

During this period I have benefited greatly from many who have shared their ideas and enthusiasms with me, both directly and through their writings. In this regard I am especially grateful to Elizabeth P. Benson, Michael D. Coe, Tom D. Dillehay, Marion Oettinger, Stephen Hugh-Jones, Jay Kettle-Williams, Gerardo Reichel-Dolmatoff and Peter J. Ucko. Their scholarship and critical insights have profoundly affected my own thinking, though in no sense can they be held responsible for many of the views expressed in this book.

Special thanks are due to Jaime Litvak who, whilst Director of the Instituto de Investigaciones Antropologicas at Mexico's National Autonomous University (UNAM), along with the British Council, enabled me to spend an invaluable year in Mexico from 1981–2. During this time I visited many of that country's great archaeological sites and observed at first hand the 'jaguar festival' of Acatlán in the state of Guerrero. The British Academy and Southampton University made possible my attendance at the 46th International Congress of Americanists in Amsterdam in 1988, at which several of the ideas in this book were first presented to a scholarly audience.

To my parents I am grateful for instilling a youthful interest in archaeology during countless weekends spent exploring the hillforts and prehistoric monuments of 'Wessex'. Such formative experiences, along with extended periods of family travel and residence abroad, led to an early appreciation that the past is indeed another country, where people do things differently. In addition, the longstanding personal friendships of the following have been and continue to be greatly valued: William Chandler, Robert Craig, Steve Cunliffe, François Philippe Reeve, Sonia Rivero, Barry Shea, Keith Stringfellow and John Wyatt.

Above all, thanks go to Pauline, my wife, without whose patient support and encouragement this book could never have been written. Her many drawings have made the book more interesting and informative than it would otherwise have been. Tessa Harrow, my editor at Souvenir Press, was a model of forbearance during the long process of writing.

I would like to thank the following for permission to quote from copyright material: Temple University Press for *The Shaman and the Jaguar* by G. Reichel-Dolmatoff, Copyright © 1975, reprinted by permission of Temple University Press; University of Illinois Press for *The Cubeo* by I. Goldman (2nd ed.), 1979; University of Texas Press for *In the Land of the Olmec* by M. D. Coe and R. A. Diehl, Copyright © 1980; Penguin Books Ltd for *Shamanic Voices* by J. Halifax, 1979; Doubleday & Co. Inc. for *The Jivaro* by M. J. Harner, 1973; and Macmillan Company Inc. for *Mexico South* by M. Covarrubius, 1946. Reproduced by permission of the Smithsonian Institution Press, are quotations from *Excavations at La Venta, Tabasco, 1955* by Philip Drucker, Robert F. Heizer and Robert J. Squier, Bureau of American Ethnology, Bulletin 170, 1959, Smithsonian Institution, Washington D.C. pp. 93–94; and also reproduced by permission of the Smithsonian Institution Press, from *Handbook of South American Indians: The Comparative Ethnology of South American Indians* (Vol. 5), edited by Julian H. Steward, Bureau of American Ethnology, Bulletin 143, 1949. Smithsonian Institution, Washington D.C. p. 596. Quotations from *Tribes and Temples*, by F. Blom and O. La Farge, 1926–7, are reproduced courtesy of the Middle American Research Institute, Tulane University, New Orleans, LA.

Finally, I would like to thank the staff of the Haddon Library, Cambridge, and Southampton University Library, especially Teresa Russell, Joan Chapman and Anne Marie McCann of the Inter-Library Loans service, all of whom have greatly facilitated the researching of this book.

CONTENTS

LIST OF ILLUSTRATIONS

INTRODUCTION

The continents of North and South America, whose ancient heritage has only in the last hundred years begun to emerge from the shadows, are guardians of a mystery that has enthralled their peoples throughout their long history. Among the abandoned ruins of a forgotten past lurk tenacious beliefs in the existence of sorcerers, the reality of magic and the potent image of the jaguar.

Isolated from the continents of Europe and Asia, the mighty empires of the Aztecs and Incas, so swiftly overthrown by the Spanish explorers, gave no clue to their conquerors that they were but the last in a long line of Pre-Columbian civilisations stretching back thousands of years. Yet the secret of their inheritance was all around, in their temples and rituals, in their beliefs and symbols of power.

Buried deep in tropical rainforests, arid deserts and remote mountain valleys, archaeologists have uncovered a dazzling array of remains which bear silent witness to the strange and distant cultures of Ancient America; pervading them all is the same, compelling symbol. Cast in gold, carved in stone or colourfully portrayed in cave paintings and textiles, the feline image has been a recurring motif for more than three thousand years. From the swamps of eastern Mexico and the high Andes of Peru come monumental stone sculptures, jaguar emblems of rulership and dynastic succession, feline images that once watched over ceremonies celebrating the narcotic coca leaf, ritual head-hunting and human sacrifice.

Amazingly, the mystery of the jaguar did not die with the last Pre-Columbian empires. Modern clues to the meaning of those age-old beliefs lie with the still surviving peoples of the Amazonian rainforest. The Stone Age inhabitants of this jungle universe believe in the existence of a mirrored realm of spirit-beings, the power of ancestors and the magical threat of sorcery. Here, where the boundary between humans and animals is blurred and sorcerers deal in 'magical death', the jaguar is revealed as an omnipotent force—an untamed manifestation of natures's raw power.

Powerful and evocative, the spirit of the jaguar offers a fascinating thread of culture which binds us to the prehistoric past in a kaleidoscope of ancient mythical images and modern survivals. Symbol of royalty and priestly power, master of animals and ruler of the underworld, the soul of the jaguar is a living force which has endured from the time of the Olmec in the second millennium BC, right down to our own era.

Tracing the appearance and decoding the significance of jaguar symbolism is the central theme of this book—a theme which occupies the fertile ground between archaeology and anthropology. It takes us on a journey through time, space and human perception, whose aim is to shed light on the mysteries of the past by seeking to understand those of the present.

CHAPTER 1

A NEW WORLD

On 30 April, 1492, Christopher Columbus, a Genoese of humble birth, received an extraordinary royal patent from King Ferdinand and Queen Isabella of Spain. On behalf of the Spanish Crown he was to discover and take possession of 'certain islands and *Tierra Firme*' far to the west in the Ocean Sea—today's Atlantic Ocean. His fleet was to consist of three ships—the *Santa María, Niña* and *Pinta*. Whilst the last two vessels were to be crewed by experienced seamen, many of whom were kinsmen of Columbus's second in command, Martin Alonso Pinzón, the flagship *Santa María* would be manned with prisoners judiciously offered an amnesty if they volunteered to join the expedition.

The full terms of Columbus's patent were astounding: he was to be the Admiral, Viceroy and Governor of all the lands he discovered; by virtue of any successes, he was to enter the Spanish gentility and be called Don Christopher Columbus; and, perhaps most surprising of all, his titles and privileges were to be considered hereditary, assumed by his sons and successors 'forever and always'. In addition, he was to keep no less than ten per cent of all the wealth he discovered.

Columbus and his small flotilla set sail on 3 August, 1492, from the Atlantic Spanish port of Palos. Seven days later they reached the Canaries, where they spent a month taking on water and provisions, and on 8 September, with a north-east wind, they set off across the uncharted Ocean Sea. After some eleven days, at two hours after midnight on 12 October, land was sighted. The following morning, in the name of the Spanish Crown, Columbus took possession of a small island which he named San Salvador. Today many experts agree that this first landfall was Watling's Island in the Bahamas. However, recent investigations indicate that Columbus may actually have landed on Samana Cay, some 60 nautical miles south-east of Watling's Island. It had taken this small expedition only 33 days to cross the Atlantic and make one of the most momentous discoveries in history.

Columbus mistakenly called the brown-skinned inhabitants of his island 'Indians', but in reality they were a simple people known today as Arawaks, one of two ethnic groups in the islands, the other being called Caribs. A mixture of justification for conquest and the Arawaks' dislike of their more warlike neighbours soon led to these Carib peoples being referred to in increasingly derogatory terms. The very name became corrupted to Canibs and thence Cannibals, and by the time Columbus returned to Spain they were credited, possibly quite erroneously, with the gruesome habit of eating not only their enemies but their own kind as well.

After spending some little time amongst the friendly Arawaks of San Salvador and several adjacent Bahamian islands, Columbus, now entitled to the grand title Admiral of the Ocean Sea and Viceroy of the Indies, concluded that, apart from a few pieces of native jewellery, there were no great sources of gold to be found in these small coral islands. He moved on, arriving in Cuba on 28 October—only to be disappointed once again with the primitive inhabitants, the jagged coastline, an obvious lack of great cities and the equally obvious dearth of gold. Further south, he was told, there were indeed people who wore great quantities of the precious metal, so he left Cuba after only four days, moving south-eastwards across the Windward Passage that separates Cuba from Hispaniola (modern Haiti and Dominican Republic).

If Cuba had been a disappointment, Hispaniola was more to his liking. Sailing along its northern coast and noting its green and fertile land, the expedition met with Guacanagari, a major Arawakan chief. His subjects came aboard the Spanish ships, trading food and other goods for objects of Spanish iron and bronze. It was here, whilst being lavishly entertained by their Amerindian hosts, that the Spaniards caught their first substantial glimpse of gold. Many of Guacanagari's lesser chiefs wore thin sheets of the precious metal in their finery, and the Europeans learned of the alluvial source of this gold, which was apparently washed down from mountain streams in an area known as *Cibao*. A few weeks later Martín Alonso Pinzón reported that he had penetrated some 50 miles inland and had reached these golden lands.

Throughout his sojourn in the West Indies Columbus constantly heard of gold-using peoples, always to the east or south; just as with the later legend of El Dorado in South America, the natives had probably realised exactly what the Spaniards' motivation was, and consequently gave them the answer they desired but always 'over there', never nearby. A land rich in gold was a concept implanted in the minds of Columbus and his men long before their arrival in the West Indies. Indeed, Columbus apparently shared the common belief that gold was generated by heat and thus associated with hot places. As with all the early European discoverers and conquistadores, it came as a rude awakening to discover that there was a great difference between naturally occurring pure gold and the ornaments of shiny yellow metal worn by the natives, which were often a mixture of gold and copper, referred to as *tumbaga*.

Just before Christmas 1492, to the east of Cap Haïtien, Columbus's flagship the *Santa María* struck a reef and sank. With the stray planks salvaged from the wreckage a rough and ready blockhouse was built and christened *Navidad*. This was the first European settlement in the West Indies and was manned by about forty of Columbus's men, who were left with the Admiral's orders to plant crops and search for gold. Navidad and its reluctant inhabitants did not survive the year.

With the *Santa María* lost and the other two ships in need of overhaul, Columbus decided to sail for Spain with the news of his dramatic discoveries. He embarked on 16 January from the Bay of Samaná and reached Lisbon on 4 March, 1493. Eleven days later he entered Palos. His epic journey had taken six months.

In April he was welcomed at a state reception in Barcelona, where the royal court was then established. A letter sent by Columbus to Ferdinand and Isabella from Lisbon was translated into Latin, French, German and Italian, ran to seventeen editions and quickly became a sensation. Columbus's titles were confirmed, while in Rome Papal bulls were issued by Pope Alexander VI, stating explicitly that these new discoveries were Spanish possessions and that the Spanish Crown had a right and a duty to bring these new peoples to the Catholic faith.

Thus was America discovered. Several further expeditions took Columbus back to the West Indies, along the coastlines of *Tierra Firme*—today the Caribbean shores of Honduras, Nicaragua and Costa Rica. These exploratory forays led to the colonisation of the islands of the West Indies, and eventually to the Spanish conquest of Mexico under Hernán Cortés, between 1519 and 1521, and of Peru by Francisco Pizarro in 1532. With a mixture of experience, foresight, greed and mystical inspiration, Christopher Columbus had brought to an end thousands of years of cultural and geographical isolation for America's indigenous inhabitants.

The First Americans

In 1492 Europeans had accidentally stumbled across the Caribbean Islands, outliers of a hitherto unsuspected New World—a vast continent populated by perhaps 20 million people. The initial European incursions discovered small and relatively simple tribal societies but no great cities, no vast riches of precious stones or hoards of gold and silver. In many ways the only tangible resources were the natives themselves, and the often rich and fertile lands which they inhabited. But the conquistadores arrived in increasing numbers, and it was only a matter of time before greater discoveries were made— discoveries which challenged the intellectual minds of Europe as well as filling the coffers of the Spanish Crown.

Unlike the small communities of the Caribbean, the Aztecs of Mexico and Incas of Peru were huge, tightly run states: they lived in cities, had standing armies, practised a highly organised if 'obviously pagan' religion, and pos- sessed a wide range of sophisticated arts and crafts. Who were these native Americans and where could they have come from? In Europe speculation was rife, and imagination was fuelled when Columbus showed off his 'Indians' in Spain, when fifty Brazilian Indians appeared at the court of King Henri II of France at Rouen in 1550, and when strange but beautifully wrought objects of silver, gold and feathers arrived back in Europe as the first booty of conquest.

Most theories concerning the origins of the Amerindians relied on the

Monumental Inca masonry frames a giant stairway giving access to the huge fortress of Sacsahuaman which overlooked the Inca capital of Cuzco. *Photo, Author*

biblical and classical sources available in Europe. Proponents argued that the Americas had been colonised by Carthaginians some 2,000 years before Columbus, or that their inhabitants were intimately connected with the lost continent of Atlantis or the exiled Ten Tribes of Israel. Despite a plethora of exotic ideas, none were or could be truly objective—all were firmly locked into the narrow view of the world as seen from late fifteenth- and sixteenth-century Europe. It was the Jesuit priest, José de Acosta, who in 1589 suggested, with some prescience, that America's native inhabitants had first reached the New World from Asia by land and possibly sea. At this early date there was no knowledge of the proximity of the American and Asian landmasses far to the north, where Siberia confronts Alaska across only 50 miles of shallow, icy sea. Another 140 years were to pass before the Russian explorer, Vitus Bering, discovered the narrow straits which now bear his name.

Today archaeologists still speculate on the origins of native Americans, but in more informed and less fanciful terms. Until the middle of the 1960s it was commonly accepted that the earliest dates for man in the Americas centred around the period between 11,000 and 10,000 years ago. A wealth of well documented and securely dated sites and objects were ascribed to two Stone Age cultures, Clovis and Folsom. In 1927, at Folsom in New Mexico, distinctively fluted stone blades were found *in situ* within the rib cage of an extinct Ice Age bison. Two decades later, further investigations at the site revealed another similar but equally distinctive type of stone blade beneath the Folsom levels: this was labelled the Clovis culture. With the development of the

Cross-section view of the remains of the Great Aztec Temple, Mexico City. Note the seven stone statues found *in situ* and the difference in street levels of the Aztec capital and the Spanish city. *Photo, Author*

revolutionary radiocarbon dating technique in 1949, a truly objective assessment of such finds was possible and the mounting evidence indicated dates for the Clovis culture around 11,000 BP (before present) and the succeeding Folsom culture a thousand years later.

In the 1960s, however, dramatic and contentious discoveries were made which suggested to some that man had been in the Americas by at least 30,000 BP and possibly much earlier. In 1966 investigations in the redeposited and confusing strata at Old Crow in Canada's Yukon territory revealed an obviously worked caribou bone shaped into what has been called a flesher, and a number of mammoth bones which the investigators interpreted as artefacts, due to the distinctive spiral fractures revealed by micro-analysis. The flesher yielded a date of 27,000 BP and the other bones dates around 30,000 BP. For many years this discovery was regarded by many as a watershed, strongly suggestive of man's presence in the Americas much earlier than 11,000 years ago.

Grave doubts have now arisen concerning these finds, as the flesher has been recently re-dated to c. 1,300 BP, and the debate still rages as to whether or not the more ambiguous mammoth bones are the work of man or natural forces. However, as the primacy of Old Crow has receded, other sites have been discovered which continue to suggest dates preceding the Clovis people. 'Meadowcroft' rockshelter in the United States, and the recently documented cave site of 'Boquerião de Pedra Furada' in Brazil—with dates spanning the period between 30,000 and 20,000 years ago—have joined other disputedly early sites such as Tlapacoya in the valley of Mexico (c. 21,000 BP) and Pikimachay Cave in the Peruvian Andes (c. 20,000 BP). Nevertheless, whilst the dating of early man in the Americas is divided between the early but ambiguous sites and the later and well documented ones, it does seem as if the 11,000 BP barrier has been breached. Dates between 12,000 and 14,000 BP at such sites as Monte Verde in Chile and Bluefish Caves in Canada now appear to be firmly established. It seems that the ancestors of America's indigenous inhabitants may have crossed the land bridge known as Beringia, which joined the Asian and American continents, by at least 15,000 BP, gradually making their way south to colonise North, Central and finally South America.

From Hunters to Farmers

Whatever the exact date for early man's arrival in the Americas, there is no doubt that around 10,000 years ago there was a dramatic change in climate as temperatures rose and the ice sheets of the Wisconsin withdrew from vast tracts of North America. For the big game hunters of the Americas this change signalled a reorientation in their way of life: increasing emphasis was placed on gathering wild plant foods and hunting smaller animals such as deer, gophers and rabbits. Whilst the gathering of wild plants had always been an important supplement to the meat diet, between about 7,000 and 2,000 BC small human groups came to rely on and experiment increasingly with this resource, and to develop what we term agriculture. In the Tehuacán valley, south of Mexico City, the North American archaeologist Richard MacNeish has made extensive investigations into the slow but significant shift away from hunting large game to 'managing' the land and producing domesticated food rather than hunting it 'on the hoof'.

The evidence from Tehuacán and elsewhere in the Americas indicates that the cultivation of Chili peppers, avocado, amaranth and maize brought about a great change in the patterns and conditions of everyday life in this important transitional stage of cultural development. Small human groups became less nomadic, staying for longer periods in one place, and began developing specialisations such as house building and pottery manufacture. Perhaps as early as 6,000 BC the shamans or medicine men of the earlier hunting tribes began to extend their spirit-derived power and influence to cover the benefits of agriculture and a village way of life.

The consequences of this new, more settled living pattern were dramatic. Staying put for increasingly longer periods of time probably had a significant effect both on the birth-rate, with more babies and mothers surviving the initial trauma, and on the longevity of adults. Pottery, an all but useless burden to mobile hunters, became a virtual necessity for storage in agricultural villages, and the organisation and mobilisation of people to plant, tend and harvest the crops demanded new systems of control. Moreover, it was now the land itself rather than the passing game which was of utmost importance, and so notions of territorialism, or possession and defence of land, developed. Agriculture brought with it a whole new array of attitudes and ideas in human societies and these laid the foundations for the arrival of sophisticated civilisations.

We should remember that, whilst archaeologists evaluate agriculture and its new way of life as crucial to the development of civilisation, it did not occur everywhere, nor, in places where it did occur, did it develop at the same time or the same rate. Some environments, such as the north-west coast of North America, were so rich in natural resources like fish, game and wild plants that there was no spur to develop agriculture at all. In other parts of the Americas as well, there was no crucial mix of necessity and social motivation which would lead to agriculture; hunting and gathering persisted in such areas right down to the European discovery in the fifteenth century and, in some places, to the present day.

The development of agriculture was less a case of revolution than of evolution. Once the change had been made, however, labour resources could as easily be directed to building ceremonial or secular buildings as to managing an agricultural system. Once populations had begun to increase and societies developed beyond the point of no return, the social foundations for true civilisation had been laid. It was arguably only a matter of time before some places saw the arrival of civilisation itself. Whilst it is not the aim of this book to chronicle in any depth the range and achievements of all the Pre-Columbian civilisations, a brief account will serve as a useful framework for our main theme.

Ancient Mexico

Civilisation in Mexico began with the Olmec culture, around 1250 BC. As we shall see in the following chapters, the Olmecs created a precocious and sophisticated culture which many believe to have laid the religious, ideological and economic foundations for all succeeding civilisations. For the first time in Mexico there appeared impressive ceremonial centres, adorned with a startling array of monumental stone sculpture, itself decorated in a distinctive art style which blended the real and the imaginary. Supported by a dispersed rural population, great Olmec centres such as San Lorenzo and La Venta were built as sacred places to the supreme deities which, due to the very primacy of the Olmec, had much in common with the gods and spirits of earlier hunting and gathering societies.

Olmec rulers, perhaps regarded as semi-divine descendants of mythical ancestors, had their likenesses carved in gigantic stone heads, and their 'cities', perhaps seen as the earthly abodes of the gods, were thoughtfully laid out and carefully planned for the maximum political and psychological effect. Under the royal patronage of all-powerful rulers, Olmec civilisation produced some of the finest jadework ever seen in the Americas; they built ancient Mexico's first pyramid and engaged in long-distance trade across Mexico to gather the precious greenstones so important in their ritual life.

Olmec culture ushered in an age of sophisticated civilisation and their, to us, strange religious beliefs centred around a fierce and impressive feline deity—the jaguar. On pottery, jade, stone sculpture and cave murals feline symbolism was ever present, signifying perhaps a concept of divine rulership. Around 400 BC, however, the Olmec declined and the focus of Mexican civilisation shifted to the valley of Oaxaca in central southern Mexico.

Between the period 1200 and 900 BC, the early site of San José Mogote had also seen precocious cultural development. Situated in the Etla valley, one of three small valleys making up the Oaxaca valley system, San José Mogote's artisans had produced iron-ore mirrors for the great Gulf Coast Olmec centres and had received some Olmec influence in return. However, it was the period between 500 BC and AD 750 that saw the greatest achievements of this part of Mexico—in the form of the great political centre of Monte Albán.

Situated some 400 metres above the valley floor at a point where all three sub-valleys met, Monte Albán became a hugely impressive and architecturally distinctive regional capital, dominated by a series of much rebuilt temples surrounding a large ceremonial plaza. Early on, people from the surrounding valleys moved up to the hill-top site, creating an estimated resident population of between 10,000 and 15,000. At this time the famous 'Danzante' figures were carved in low relief on stone slabs. They depicted nude and mutilated captives in a gruesome iconography of military power and human sacrifice. Even at this early time the inhabitants were using a system of bars and dots to record dates in their 260-day ritual calendar.

At its peak, between AD 300 and 750, Monte Albán housed perhaps 25,000

A 'Danzante' figure from the main plaza at the Zapotec capital of Monte Albán, Oaxaca.
Photo, Author

people and extended over some six square kilometres. During the last great building phase, a huge pyramid, some 15 metres high, was erected and was flanked by carved stelae at each of its four sides. The figures carved onto these monolithic slabs apparently commemorated a visit to Monte Albán by an 'ambassador' from the other great metropolis of the time, Teotihuacán. Around AD 750 Monte Albán went into decline and its concentrated population dispersed along the three sub-valleys whence their predecessors had originally come, more than a thousand years before.

At the same time as Monte Albán was flourishing in southern Mexico, a greater civilisation was developing some way to the north. Feeding into the great Basin of Mexico is a small valley dominated by the huge metropolis of Teotihuacán. Between the time of Christ and *c.* AD 650 Teotihuacán was the single most important city in Mexico, a magnet for population and a giant pre-industrial city.

The sheer scale of Teotihuacán is staggering, with a mass of ceremonial and more humble buildings extending over an area of some 22 square kilometres—the total population of the city may have been as high as 200,000. Dominating the site is a densely packed cluster of monumental architecture ranged on either side of a north–south avenue known as the 'Street of the Dead'. The basis of Teotihuacán's economic power and influence was undoubtedly its control of obsidian, a volcanic glass that was the 'steel of prehistory'. The manufacture and distribution of finished obsidian tools made Teotihuacán the dominant centre for economic and religious power in central Mexico.

The grand architecture at Teotihuacán is what impresses most. At the northern end of the Street of the Dead is the so-called Pyramid of the Moon, set in a spacious plaza and flanked by smaller temple-pyramids. At the southern end is the great compound known as the Ciudadela, which encompasses the Temple of Quetzalcóatl with its distinctive stone carvings of feathered serpents. The most striking building by far, however, is the huge Pyramid of the Sun,

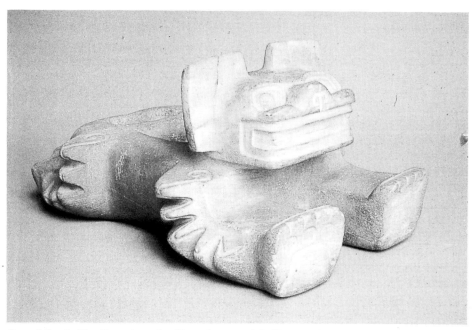

Onyx feline in Teotihuacán style. *Photo, Courtesy of the Trustees of the British Museum*

built over a series of natural caves in which has been found evidence of ceremonial activity. Teotihuacán, with its concentration of pyramid-temples, massive architecture, high-walled house compounds and unique, brightly coloured murals, dominated the physical and cultural landscape of central Mexico for some 700 years. Around AD 650 there was a great conflagration from which the city never recovered. Its collapse may have prompted the demise of Monte Albán to the south, but it was also an early herald of the demise of the Classic Period in Mexico's prehistory.

Shrouded today in the deepest recesses of the tropical rainforests of Mexico, Guatemala, Honduras and Belize are the testaments to the genius of the Classic Maya civilisation. Flourishing between AD 300 and 900 this strange culture was never an empire but rather a number of autonomous city-states, much like Classical Athens. The ruling dynasties of each Maya city were regarded as having a divine ancestry, and they entered into constantly shifting systems of alliances, punctuated by gruesome blood sacrifices and elaborate pomp and ceremony which accompanied the accession to power of new rulers.

All Maya cities, however, shared the same characteristic features. Often regarded as the intellectuals of Pre-Columbian America, the Classic Maya had a complex dual calendar system, a hieroglyphic script and a counting system which had mastered the concept of zero. As a strictly hierarchical society, the great cultural achievements of the Maya were essentially restricted to the elite—the royal family, retainers, scribes and priests; the mass of the population were agricultural labourers and makers of everyday tools and pottery.

The 'Palace' structure at the Maya centre of Palenque. *Photo, Author*

Great dynastic cities such as Tikal, El Mirador, Palenque, Copán, Seibal and Uxmal, all possessed elaborately planned and built ceremonial architecture, pyramids which often served as both mausoleums for the deified dead and temples for the living, and a host of carved stone stelae—essentially propaganda monuments extolling the virtues of the city's rulers. Maya civilisation may well have been the product of cultural 'hot-housing'—the sheer density, richness and frequency of interaction creating a highly distinctive brand of culture.

However, between AD 800 and 900 Classic Maya civilisation collapsed. There is no generally accepted explanation for this, and the theories put forward range from social unrest and agricultural failure to outside interference from central Mexico. With the demise of the Maya the Classic Period truly comes to an end and the so-called Postclassic period is ushered in.

The two greatest civilisations of this final period of Mexican prehistory are the Toltecs and Aztecs. Between around AD 950 and 1150 a new outlook was engendered in the peoples of central Mexico—that of militarism, large-scale blood sacrifice and imperial conquest. At their hastily constructed capital of Tula, north-west of Mexico City, the Toltecs built a centre dominated today by the reconstructed temple-pyramid of Quetzalcóatl (the Feathered Serpent), two large ball-courts and a great central plaza. Investigations have shown that the Toltecs engaged in long-distance trade, perhaps to the cacao-rich Pacific coastal regions and the lush jungles of Veracruz to the east. These extensive connections with other parts of greater Mesoamerica may well account for the appearance in Mexico at this time of the metalsmith's art.

Tula's architectural legacy includes dramatic scenes of supposed human sacrifice and warrior societies of the Eagle and Jaguar. A decorative panel on the pyramid of Quetzalcóatl shows marching lines of jaguars or pumas and eagles consuming human hearts. There is little doubt that the Toltecs are the prime example of the new spirit of Postclassic Mexico, but their reign, if not their influence, was short lived. By AD 1150 Tula was essentially abandoned and this whole region of central Mexico underwent a process of Balkanisation from which it emerged only with the appearance of the imperial Aztecs.

The Aztecs were originally a group of wandering peoples who, according to myth, migrated from the northern marches southwards to the Valley of Mexico around AD 1325. Finding this rich area already occupied by petty states which traced their origins back to the Toltecs, the Aztecs were constantly moved on from city to city. In 1345 they established their own capital on an unprepossessing marshy island in Lake Texcoco and from here, through a series of political manoeuvres, they began their rise to an imperial civilisation.

Together with the cities of Texcoco and Tlacopan, the Aztecs formed a Triple Alliance which soon controlled the whole of the Valley of Mexico. During the 90 years between 1430 and 1520, they created the largest and most successful empire in Mexico's history—exercising their control from the sacred capital of Tenochtitlán (now Mexico City), which at its height probably housed a population of some 200,000. The vast area brought under Aztec suzerainty was less an empire than a sphere of influence, since the Aztec armies would often disregard regions which possessed either no valuable resources or a powerful native ruler. The Aztec armies themselves were far from invincible and several sources relate the difficulties encountered by their generals, especially to the west, with the peoples of the modern state of Michoacán.

Our information on the Aztecs is voluminous in comparison with their predecessors, mainly because Aztec civilisation was a 'conquest culture' and many Spanish and hybrid Aztec-Spanish sources document their lives, religious beliefs and economic organisation. In many respects we know more about Aztec culture from these colonial period Chronicles than we could ever hope to learn from archaeology alone.

Like their Postclassic predecessors the Toltecs, to whom they liked to trace their 'official origins', the Aztecs were a militaristic society. Captives taken during combat were sacrificed in vast numbers atop their impressive pyramids and the blood was considered a vital offering to their chief deity, Huitzilopochtli. Great markets, where one could barter everything from human excrement (as fertiliser) to human slaves, were regularly held and a special class of official merchants, known as *Pochteca*, played a dual role—gathering political intelligence while at the same time acquiring exotic luxuries for the burgeoning elite class of royal retainers, priests and bureaucrats.

Imposing architecture, a spectacular tradition of stone sculpture, and a

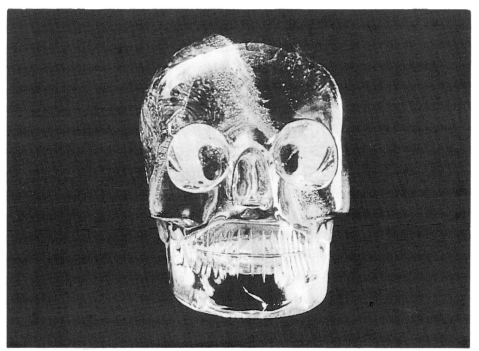

'Aztec' skull of rock crystal illustrating the Aztecs' preoccupation with death symbolism.
Photo, Courtesy of the Trustees of the British Museum

mixture of official history, myth and cosmological beliefs and rituals, provided the Aztecs with a highly visible and audible justification for their imperial ambitions. A strictly hierarchical society, with the *Tlatoani*, or First Speaker, at the apex and the commoners below, provided the framework for their economy. In 1519, some 27 years after Columbus sailed from Spain for the first time, Cortés discovered and duly conquered this last great Mexican civilisation.

Ancient Peru

In Peru civilisation probably began in the oasis-like valleys which cut across the arid coastal desert. Between around 3000 and 1000 BC massive ceremonial complexes, adorned with distinctive artistic motifs, appeared along the coastal margins. At La Florida in the Rimac valley, building was underway probably before 2150 BC, and at Sechín Alto in the Casma valley to the north, a massive building programme commenced during the Initial Period. Here, at the huge complex of Pampa de las Llamas-Moxeke, excavations have revealed a vast series of monumental mounds and administrative buildings dated to around 1400 BC. Reconstructions of Huaca A in the north-eastern part of the site show two huge jaguars, originally some six metres tall, flanking a doorway. South of the Casma valley lies another early coastal site, known as Las Haldas, and here a great stepped platform and associated buildings have been dated to between 1600 and 1400 BC.

There is little doubt that, chronologically speaking, Peruvian civilisation preceded similar developments in Mexico. Metalworking, which did not arrive in Mexico until around AD 900, had already begun in Andean South America by 1500 BC, and ceremonial centres, which in Mexico had to await the development of Olmec civilisation around 1250 BC, were already more than a thousand years old in Peru by this time.

Around 850 BC, in the northern Andes, arose the civilisation known as Chavín. Receiving cultural influences both from the great coastal centres to the west and the Amazon region to the east, the sophisticated inhabitants of Chavín de Huántar rapidly developed their 'city' into a major cult centre housing a large population divided into a wide range of craftsmen. They worked in gold, pottery, stone and textiles and were probably efficiently organised into an hierarchical society.

Dominating the site is the ceremonial architecture: the remains of elaborate pyramid structures, sunken plazas and a dramatic art style which drew its subject-matter and inspiration from the rainforests of the Amazon. At the heart of this complex but intriguing style was the image of the jaguar, sometimes rendered naturalistically but more often blended with the human form, creating a unique mythical creature which could only ever have lived in the minds of its creators. However, the jaguar motif and its significance for the Chavín culture had already been presaged by its appearance at some of the earlier coastal centres.

With the demise of Chavín around 400 BC, the focus of attention shifts once again to the Peruvian coast and the great culture of the Mochica which lasted for some 600 years, from the time of Christ to the seventh century. Here, in the valley of the River Moche whence the culture takes its name, a highly organised society developed. Today its only monumental remains are the two impressive adobe-built platforms known as the Pyramids of the Sun and the Moon, and a system of irrigation canals which once supported this militaristic state, enabling it to extend its control over several adjacent coastal valleys.

The greatest single legacy left by these coastal people, however, is a vast array of distinctive pottery. Images of everyday life, sexual behaviour and religious and mythical beliefs are all depicted in ceramic form. The range of representation is astounding, with images of confrontations between mythological creatures, men and women making *chicha* beer, fishermen at sea, elaborately garbed messengers and lifelike portraits of individuals—all possessing a distinctive stirrup-spout handle characteristic of North Coast pottery.

Flourishing at the same time as the Mochica, but this time on the southern coast of Peru, was the Nazca culture, famous for its great desert sketchboard of superimposed animal drawings and lines. Between around 200 BC and AD 650 the inhabitants of Nazca produced highly coloured pottery in a variety of naturalistic and fantastical forms. With the single exception of the political centre of Cahuachi, they apparently constructed no huge ceremonial buildings; instead they channelled their efforts into clearing vast stretches of desert pavement to produce, firstly, giant pictograms of animals such as the killer whale, spider, monkey and condor and, subsequently, a host of criss-crossing straight lines and trapezoidal plazas. Much effort has been expended in interpreting these desert drawings; whatever their real significance, they represent a unique aspect of Pre-Columbian art.

The collapse of the small but distinctive Nazca culture around AD 650 may have been prompted by the emergence of a new cultural force emanating from the Andes to the east. Centred in two places—the site of Wari in the southern Peruvian Andes, and the huge ceremonial centre of Tiwanaku on the southern shores of Lake Titicaca—this influence visibly affected the local art styles in those areas in which it held sway. A blend of Tiwanaku and Nazca pottery traditions, for instance, gave birth to a highly coloured hybrid style, and at various places in the Andes the influence of Wari left its mark with the construction of systems of 'roads'—the predecessors of the much greater imperial communication system of the Incas.

The Tiwanaku–Wari phenomenon could not maintain its momentum, however, and between 800 and 1000 smaller regional states, such as Chincha on the central coast, reasserted their political and cultural independence. Emerging once again on the northern Pacific shores of Peru, the largest of these regional states rose to prominence with a new variation of coastal civilisation. This was the gold-rich Chimú empire with its great capital of Chan-Chan in the Moche valley. From Tumbes in the north to the Rimac valley in the south, the Chimú emperors held sway over what has been called a despotic empire.

Chan-Chan reached its peak around 1450, at which time it may have had a

resident population of some 25,000 and extended over some 20 square kilometres in all. This massive pre-industrial city was in fact composed of a series of
nine great compounds or *ciudadelas*, each built by a newly incumbent emperor.
The compounds themselves varied in size but their interior plan was dictated
by the prerequisite of restricted access. It seems as if these compounds served
as the palace of the ruler in life and his mausoleum in death. Certainly much of
the interior space was designed for storage of both sacred and everyday objects.
Like its predecessors, Chimú society was characterised by severe stratification.
The state organised the construction of extensive canal irrigation systems—
including one which stretched across 84 kilometres of desert and foothills, to
the adjacent Chicama valley.

Around 1470 the Chimú empire was brought to an abrupt end with the
emergence of Pre-Columbian America's greatest empire, that of the Incas. Inca
imperialism had to grapple with the same problems encountered by the
Tiwanaku–Wari civilisation—how to conquer and maintain an empire spread
throughout the Andes and incorporating a host of different ethnic groups,
languages and religious beliefs. Inca success in this task made their civilisation
the single largest empire that Pre-Columbian America had ever witnessed.

From north to south, at its peak Inca influence extended over some 4,000
kilometres, encompassing the five modern Andean nations of Ecuador, Peru,
Bolivia, Chile and Argentina. These diverse regions were knit together by some
23,000 kilometres of 'roads' and were integrated into the imperial system by the
spread of the Inca language, *Quechua*, the efficient organisation of conquered
territories and the official cult of the deified Inca emperors, who even in death

The lost Inca city of Machu Picchu, discovered in 1911 by Hiram Bingham. Never found by
the Spanish, Machu Picchu lies complete, perched in the saddle between two Andean peaks.
Photo, Author

were regarded as exercising a strong influence over the destiny of the empire and its population of between eight and twelve million people.

Although the origins of the Inca people themselves are shrouded in myth and historical uncertainty, the records that survive suggest the establishment of a royal dynasty at Cuzco under Manco Capac around AD 1200. It was not until the victory of the first true emperor, Pachacuti, over their warlike Chanka neighbours in 1438, however, that Inca society began its imperial expansion. The momentum generated by Pachacuti was continued with equal success by his son Topa Inca (1471–93), and then by Huayna Capac (1493–1525).

Inca society, like all its pedecessors, was strictly organised; the emperor or *Sapa Inca* occupied a unique position as the head of state, and below him came the royal family, retainers, the chiefs of subjugated peoples now co-opted as 'Incas by privilege', and a number of bureaucrats and specialist craftsmen. At the bottom of the social pyramid came the great mass of agricultural peasants who, efficiently organised by their superiors, built massive cities and fortresses and transformed the Andean landscape with huge terraces upon which various foods were cultivated.

Inca society was essentially an Andean phenomenon, holding sway over large stretches of the high mountain range and adjacent coast. As with their later Spanish conquerors, the Incas never made any significant military inroads into the Amazon forests where the tribal inhabitants employed simple but effective guerrilla tactics. In 1476 the Inca armies finally defeated the Chimú empire, transporting its master goldsmiths back to Cuzco to work the precious metal which, according to Inca myth, was regarded as the 'Sweat of the Sun'. We are told that as the emperor himself was believed to be the 'Son of the Sun' all gold belonged to his royal person, just as all silver belonged to his official wife, the *Coya*.

Playing on the age-old Andean tradition of ancestor worship, the Incas created the royal cult of *Inti*, the Sun God. The empire was divided into four quarters or *suyu*, whence it derived its name *Tawantinsuyu* or the 'Land of the Four Quarters'. Official messengers or *chasqui* carried the imperial mail along the extensive road system and the records of bureaucracy were kept on a series of knotted strings or *quipu*, which acted in part as mnemonic devices. The whole empire was a tribute to the social engineering skills and foresight of the ruling dynasty and the effectiveness with which they managed both the landscape and the people of western South America.

Despite its incredible size and sophistication, in 1532 the empire succumbed to a mere handful of Spanish conquistadores led by Francisco Pizarro, and with its demise the last great Pre-Columbian civilisation disappeared and the new age of European domination began.

This brief sketch of the great achievements of America's native inhabitants serves to frame our main theme—the search for the origins of Pre-Columbian civilisation as revealed by its most prevalent symbol, the jaguar. It is to the heart of that quest that we now turn by chronicling the discovery and development of Mexico's first civilisation, the Olmec.

CHAPTER 2

THE OLMEC DISCOVERY

Spectacular archaeological discoveries only occasionally make the headlines, but when they do it is often in dramatic fashion. In 1922 Howard Carter discovered the tomb of the Egyptian boy Pharaoh Tutankhamun and, upon opening the tomb, found extraordinary riches placed inside with the mummy to accompany the dead king's soul to the other world. Whilst such a find was indicative of the pomp and ceremony of Egyptian funerary ritual, it also illustrated the wide range of craftsman's skills practised in the Egypt of the Eighteenth Dynasty. However, once the existence of the tomb was known, more peripheral aspects of the discovery stole the headlines: the 'Curse of the Pharaohs' was possibly more newsworthy than the tomb's discovery and contents. More recently, in 1974, the equally momentous discovery of the Terracotta Army, interred with the remains of the Chinese Emperor Qin Shi Huangdi at Xian, revealed the power and prestige of ancient Chinese rulers of the Chin Dynasty, their perception of the universe and the sacred nature of their political power. In both cases unexpected discoveries led to a surge of public interest and a flood of visitors—such rare events appear to strike a powerful chord in the popular imagination.

Dramatic finds in exotic places would seem for many to be the 'real stuff' of archaeology. Such a view, however, is particularly misleading, for whilst the objects themselves are of immense importance, the archaeologist seeks an overall enlightenment: a complete picture of ancient Egyptian or Chinese society is only possible if the 'context' of the discovery is known. The archaeologist must attempt to explain the nature of the society which produced such impressive burial displays and, in the final analysis, this can only be accomplished by the painstaking efforts of the trowel and brush.

Not all areas of the world elicit such an emotional response to important archaeological discoveries. In 1978 a Mexican worker, busy digging a trench for an electric cable, came across a giant stone disc carved with the figure of the decapitated Aztec Moon Goddess 'Coyolxauhqui'. Over the next few years whole streets were torn down and one of Mexico's most important excavations took place in the heart of downtown Mexico City. The discoveries at the 'Templo Mayor' site had a tremendous impact at the popular and academic levels in Mexico itself; yet when compared with the discoveries mentioned above, there was muted public interest around the world and even within the archaeological community. Adequately if somewhat selectively covered in the world's media, the excavation of the greatest Aztec temple in Mexico singularly failed to fire the public imagination, although it was of paramount significance.

Unfortunately it has been a long time since the world at large sat up and took notice of the archaeological discoveries of ancient American civilisations. During the early 1840s the trailblazing journeys through the Maya rainforests of Central America by John Lloyd Stephens and Frederick Catherwood brought to light hitherto unknown Maya cities 'lost' in the dense tropical jungles of Mexico, Guatemala and Honduras. These dramatic discoveries, and the careful way in which they were reported and illustrated, led to an understandable surge of public interest as well as a scholarly reassessment of Mexico's prehistoric past.

Comparable interest in the Inca civilisation of Peru was stimulated some seventy years later when, in 1911, a young Yale University historian, Hiram Bingham, discovered the lost Inca city of Machu Picchu, perched precipitously on a mountain top some seventy miles north of Cuzco in the heart of the Peruvian Andes. Whilst both discoveries were important, they led to an over-romanticised view of the Pre-Columbian past, where 'Lost Cities', 'Sacred Virgins' and 'incredible' feats of engineering and architecture came to the fore, pushing aside such academic interests as the nature of Maya or Inca society, their different pottery traditions, agricultural systems and cultural origins. Once again, they represented the New World's equivalent of the later dramatic discoveries in Egypt and China. Moreover, these discoveries only added information, albeit of a sensational nature, to civilisations which were already known; no new civilisation was uncovered.

In 1864 Catherwood and Stephens published their famous book, *Incidents of Travel in Central America, Chiapas and Yucatan*, describing their discoveries; the popular conception of a lost Maya civilisation, with its great cities swathed in the lush vegetation of the steaming tropical rainforests, gripped the imagination and the Maya occupied centre stage in the annals of Mexican prehistory. However, no one knew how old the Maya were, where they had come from and what part, if any, they had played in the birth of Mexican civilisation.

A New Civilisation

A true understanding of the origins of ancient Mexican society began in the middle years of the nineteenth century, accompanied by no fanfare of publicity, no surge of popular interest. In 1862 the traveller-come-explorer, José María Melgar, uncovered an archaeological enigma that was to change the face of Mexican prehistory. Travelling through the tropically humid state of Vera-cruz, whose eastern boundary was the southern shore of the Gulf of Mexico, he heard of a strange stone sculpture which had been found near the small town of Hueyapan. Deciding to investigate at first hand, he unearthed a giant monolithic stone head with no trace of either a body or an archaeological context.

As a work of art, it is, without exaggeration, a magnificent sculpture . . . but what amazed me was that the type it represents is Ethiopian. I concluded that there had doubtless been blacks in this region, and from the very earliest ages of the world.

Melgar was not an archaeologist and his opinions unconsciously reflected the intellectual atmosphere of his day. His initial statements opened the floodgates to a plethora of exotic and fantastical theories concerning 'foreign' interference in the indigenous developments of Mexican prehistory. It was far easier to explain such finds by reference to the Old World than to attempt to assign the sculpture to an original Mexican culture. Although now, over a hundred years later, we possess a much better understanding of the processes of prehistoric Mexican civilisations, echoes of such exotic speculations still abound in the extraterrestrial theories of Erich Von Däniken and his imitators.

Almost a quarter of a century after Melgar's discovery, in 1886, the Mexican archaeologist Alfredo Chavero published a picture of what was then an unusual artefact, totally unrelated to the colossal head at Hueyapan. This was a delicately carved piece of jadeite, which Chavero called a 'votive axe', decorated with an artistic motif which was to recur time and again in the recovery of what would come to be known as the Olmec civilisation. The votive axe represented a human figure with recognisably feline features, later to be called 'were-jaguar'.

In 1900 Marshall Saville published an illustration of the so-called 'Kunz axe' and commented, not for the last time, on its distinctive feline characteristics. He noted perceptively that, along with other similar specimens, such sophisticated handiwork indicated the existence of a highly distinctive and hitherto unknown art style which, for the time being, could not be assigned to any known Mexican civilisation. The mystery surrounding this unknown people deepened, but between 1900 and 1925 no serious archaeological steps were taken to investigate the supposed civilisation which had produced such unexpected and extraordinary works of art.

It was not until 1925 that a Danish archaeologist working at Tulane University in New Orleans took the first steps towards explaining the enigma posed by these isolated discoveries. Frans Blom, accompanied by an ethnographer colleague, Oliver La Farge, began scientific research in the region of Veracruz known as Los Tuxtlas, during a scientific journey which took them from eastern Mexico down into the Maya area. Whilst in Los Tuxtlas, Blom and La Farge discovered another colossal head, similar to that found by Melgar more than sixty years before.

Although eastern Mexico is largely a region of tropical forest, coastal swamps and sluggish rivers, it is dominated by an area of volcanic highlands known as the Tuxtlas. It was here, at an altitude of some 1,211 metres, at the peak of a local volcano known as San Martín Pajapan, that Blom and La Farge found a truly spectacular stone sculpture. In fact they had only rediscovered this monument, for in 1897 a Mexican engineer named Ismael Loya had

Olmec jadeite votive axe showing typical flame eyebrows, cleft forehead and snarling feline mouth. *Photo, Courtesy of the Trustees of the British Museum*

surveyed the whole region and mentioned his discovery of a strange stone idol. Although Loya had seriously damaged the statue by moving it, he did make an additional and significant discovery.

Under the figure a small pit was found in which stood some pieces of pottery containing various small objects of jade. Mr Loya had given all these away but one, which is a small piece of light green jade carved in the form of a rattlesnake.

Although Loya did not realise it at the time, his discovery was the first to prove a definite relationship between the delicately carved jades, now scattered throughout the world's museums, and the monumental stone sculptures as represented by the colossal heads. As for the San Martín Pajapan sculpture, Blom and La Farge described it thus:

The idol is squatting and according to Loya's drawing holds a bar horizontally with both hands, its body leaning forward. Arms, feet, and the bar have disappeared, and the face is badly mutilated. The total height of the figure is 1.35 metres, of which 57 cms is taken up by the headdress. The head is well carved and has large earplugs in the ears. The headdress is very elaborate. On its front is a face with slanting eyes, a small broad nose, and a downward curved mouth with a broad flaring upper lip.

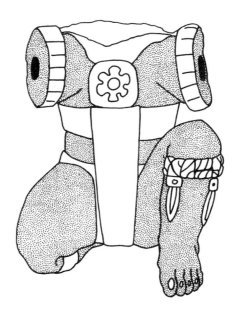

Monument 34 from San Lorenzo, showing unique kneeling figure with possible mirror pendant on his chest and shoulder sections, suggesting original moving arms. It is possible that this represents an Olmec ruler in his ritual role as a 'ball player'. *Drawing, Pauline Stringfellow, after Coe and Diehl 1980, Fig. 466*

Monument 19 from La Venta, showing an Olmec personage wearing a jaguar helmet and sitting on a supernatural serpent. *Drawing, Pauline Stringfellow, after Drucker, Heizer and Squier 1959, Fig. 55*

Both Blom and La Farge could only speculate on the figure's significance as they had no idea which of Mexico's ancient civilisations had produced it. Finding it on level ground in a saddle between the two highest points of the volcano's crater, they guessed that it might have represented a fire or mountain deity.

Continuing their journey south-east from the Tuxtlas and crossing difficult swampy country with its numerous rivers, they finally reached the drainage area of the river Tonalá and, after taking local directions, came across an 'island' surrounded on all sides by swampy land. The site was known as La Venta. Trudging through the tangled undergrowth they came across a block of carved stone decorated in relief and depicting a skirt-clad figure. A little further on they found what was later recognised to be Mexico's oldest pyramid—an earthen mound still standing some 25 metres high and enveloped in lush vegetation. It was apparent to both men that they were wandering around in the centre of a huge archaeological site whose previous existence had been unknown and whose elaborate and impressive monuments had lain hidden by the Mexican jungle for untold centuries.

More wonders were to come. Searching through the undergrowth, they uncovered a clutch of impressive stone monuments, four of which were of such a distinctive shape that they called them 'altars'.

> After our meal the guides brought us to a lot of land owned by an Indian, Leopoldo Sarabia, and here showed us another huge altar. This, altar 4, was a large square block of stone, 3.15 metres along the top, 1.90 metres deep, and with about 1.5 metres exposed above the ground. We calculated the mass of this block to be at least 9 cubic metres. On its north side is an incised ornament along the upper rim of the table, and under this is a deep niche in which sits a human figure, legs crossed Turkish fashion.

Both men could hardly appreciate the magnitude of their discoveries. Singlehandedly, they had put La Venta on the archaeological map and had unknowingly begun to dispel the aura of mystery which had surrounded what was to be recognised as the Olmec civilisation; without realising it, they had begun to piece together the complex jigsaw of Olmec culture.

With hindsight, there is little doubt that the sporadic finds of their predecessors were linked to their epoch-making discoveries at La Venta; Blom and La Farge had identified a hitherto unknown civilisation. However, as we have already seen, the archaeological community was held in thrall by the baroque vestiges of Classic Maya civilisation and both Blom and La Farge had no doubt in assigning the newly uncovered monuments to this great culture. Such was the strength of ideological commitment that the true significance of their discoveries eluded them.

In 1926 an account of their journey was published in an entertaining and fascinating travelogue entitled *Tribes and Temples*. A year later the book was reviewed by a German scholar named Hermann Beyer, who then made his own timely contribution to the saga. Noticing that the stone statue found by Blom and La Farge atop the San Martín Pajapan volcano was similar in general appearance to a greenstone figure formerly in his possession, he referred to these artefacts as of 'Olmec' or Totonac origin. This was the first time that the term 'Olmec' had entered the archaeological literature.

In fact, like so many aspects of the Olmec story, even the naming of it was accidental. The hot and swampy Gulf Coast region of eastern Mexico was known during Aztec times as *Olman* or 'rubber country', and its inhabitants, naturally enough, as *Olmeca*—people of the rubber country. Thus the Aztec name for a native people called after a product of their region was applied to a much earlier culture that was to become recognised as Mexico's first true civilisation. Once used, the name Olmec proved impossible to dislodge.

In 1929 Marshall Saville published two articles on the so-called 'votive axes' and used Beyer's term 'Olmec' to describe them. Saville was particularly fascinated by the peculiar appearance, both in the stone sculptures and the smaller jades, of what he perceived as feline characteristics, and he referred to them as 'tiger-faces' or 'were-jaguar' axes. It was he who first suggested that such depictions represented a jaguar god; indeed he went further by suggesting that the monstrous deity carved on such Olmec pieces represented an ancestor of the later Aztec deity Tezcatlipoca who, in one of this guises, was recognised as a jaguar. For the first time, but not for the last, the ethno-historical evidence of a later civilisation was used to look backwards in time to explain the form, appearance and significance of an earlier culture's art and, by extension, its mythological and religious beliefs.

In the decade between 1920 and 1930 the archaeological evidence for recognising the importance of the newly named Olmec civilisation broadened considerably. During this time the famous archaeologist George Vaillant, who had been conducting important excavations in the Valley of Mexico, remarked on the jade and ceramic artefacts which were emerging from the earliest levels of his excavations. He noted their similarity with other pieces recently called Olmec and duly assigned his finds to that culture. This was a significant step forward for Olmec archaeology, because hitherto all the firm evidence had come from the tropical region of eastern Mexico. Now here were indications that the Olmecs, whoever they were, had exercised a cultural influence on Mexican civilisation far beyond their immediate hinterland.

Also around this time, the well known Mexican art historian Miguel Covarrubius, understandably attracted to the distinctive Olmec style, began collecting a variety of Olmec works of art (later to be selectively published in his beautifully illustrated books on Mexico). It was Covarrubius who pointed out for the first time that many of the Olmec greenstone artefacts emanated not from the tropical east coast, but rather from the isolated and difficult terrain of Mexico's mountainous state of Guerrero, which was bordered by the Pacific Ocean to the west. Here were two indications that the Olmecs had far-flung 'contacts' with distant parts of Mexico.

Throughout the 1930s sporadic evidence continued to appear, supporting the theory of a little known but highly advanced civilisation. Many experts, such as Zelia Nuttall, Franz Boas, Eduard Seler and Herbert Spinden, had previously inferred its existence but were unable to be specific. The evidence trickled in from various regions of Mexico, many famous for later and better known civilisations. The scene was rapidly being set for all of these diverse reports and strands of evidence to be drawn together in the most dramatic fashion.

The Arrival of Olmec Archaeology

In 1920, during a visit to the Berlin Museum, a scholar named Matthew Stirling had seen a blue-jade maskette of a so-called 'Crying Baby' which he had first glimpsed in a photograph published by the Smithsonian Institution in 1898. Like so many before him, Stirling had been fascinated by the appearance and style of the piece; subsequently he found several other similar examples in

Example of Olmec carved jadeite plaque from unknown site. Note the multiple representations of the drooping feline mouth in profile on the cheek and headdress. *Drawing, Pauline Stringfellow, after Drucker, Heizer and Squier 1959, Fig. 36b*

both Vienna and Madrid. In the following year he joined the staff of the Smithsonian, discovered more apparently similar pieces in the US National Museum and, after talking to Marshall Saville, decided to investigate this still unknown civilisation.

In 1938 Stirling began his archaeological investigations in what was now acknowledged to be the Olmec heartland of southern Veracruz in eastern Mexico. Up until that time the area had been significant only inasmuch as it formed the western margins of the Maya culture area. He went into the field with the prestigious backing of the Smithsonian Institution, the National Geographic Society and the co-operation of the Mexican National Institute of History and Anthropology (INAH).

Starting his work at Hueyapan, now recognised as an archaeological site and called Tres Zapotes, Stirling and his co-worker, Clarence Weiant, soon discovered an extraordinary stone monument, now famous as 'Stela C'. On one side there was a typically Olmec face of a stylised jaguar, and on the other, incredibly, a so-called Long Count date more usually found among the later Classic Maya. When deciphered it read 7.16.6.16.18 which, when correlated with the Gregorian calendar, yielded a date of 31 BC. In fact a more elaborate version of the Long Count system was known to belong to the Maya civilisation and the Stela C date was of a simpler form, without the typical Maya hieroglyphs. Nevertheless it was an outstanding discovery.

Stirling's initial foray into the field of Olmec archaeology had uncovered the use of a numerical system outside the Maya heartland, along with an astonishingly early date. The Classic Maya did not begin their rise to civilisation until *c.* AD 250 and so the Tres Zapotes date of 31 BC was guaranteed to raise the hackles of the powerful Maya lobby amongst New World archaeologists, at that time dominated by the North Americans. Today such a date is known to be late rather than early for the Olmec, but at that time it amounted to virtual archaeological heresy. As might have been expected, Stirling's discovery and his reading of the Long Count date on Stela C caused a storm of academic debate and not a little rancour. Famous Mayanists, such as the British-born Eric Thompson, argued strongly that what Stirling called Olmec was in fact a much later civilisation belonging to the Postclassic period of Mexico's prehistory, i.e. between *c.* AD 900 and 1520. He contended that the Olmec could not possibly be earlier than his beloved Maya and was supported in this view by a large number of Mayanists. However, Mexican archaeologists and experts such as Alfonso Caso and Miguel Covarrubius, as well as Matthew Stirling himself, disagreed, firmly believing that the Olmec predated the Maya and that significant parts of Mexico's prehistory had to be rewritten. With the arrival of the new radiocarbon dating technique, the intuition of Stirling and the Mexicans was proved to be correct.

Despite the dramatic start to his investigations, Stirling was not content to rest his case with the extraordinary but singular evidence from Tres Zapotes. Whilst work continued at that site, he visited La Venta, scene of the earlier discoveries of Blom and La Farge. Upon excavating part of this site he brought to light a host of Olmec artefacts, including four more colossal stone heads. Without doubt the work at La Venta provided some of the most magnificent stone sculptures yet found in the Olmec area. One of Stirling's discoveries was Altar no. 5 which, whilst similar in shape to those found by Blom and La Farge, had as its focal point a seated figure holding a baby located in a niche at the front of the monument. This central figure was surrounded by five were-jaguar baby figures carved in bas-relief and showing typically half-human, half-feline features. Another important monument found at La Venta was called by Stirling 'Stela 3'—a large block of stone depicting two figures facing each other, each adorned with elaborate headgear.

Stirling's work at La Venta eventually uncovered the famous pyramidal mound, now known to be Mexico's first man-made pyramid—albeit of soil rather than cut stone. When he placed the pyramid in the overall context of the site, he realised that La Venta was a large planned 'ceremonial centre', strewn with impressive stone sculptures, often relating strange scenes from Olmec mythology. Taken together with the colossal heads, jade votive axes, so-called 'mirrors' made of magnetite, carved stelae and, significantly, huge buried caches of carved serpentine blocks, it was clear that the Olmec had been one of Mexico's greatest civilisations, the scale of whose cultural achievements had hitherto been unrecognised.

Whilst the investigations at La Venta continued, Mexican archaeologists organised a Round Table Conference at Tuxtla Gutiérrez in the southern Mexican state of Chiapas. Stirling spared time to attend and brought some of his latest finds from La Venta. As the conference progressed it became increasingly obvious to all that the concept of an Olmec art style (so long the only indication of the hitherto unknown civilisation) was rapidly evolving into the concept of an Olmec culture. It was equally obvious that the term 'Olmec' was a serious misnomer and that the much later historical people to whom it more accurately referred had no connection whatsoever with the considerably more ancient Olmec civilisation. However, the name had become firmly entrenched in the archaeological literature and proved impossible to change. It was at the Tuxtla conference that Alfonso Caso first called the Olmec the 'Mother Culture' of all subsequent Mexican civilisations, including the more famous Aztecs, Maya, Zapotecs and Teotihuacanos.

Irrefutable evidence which was acceptable to the archaeological community at large, and which settled the dating problem once and for all, came in 1955, with the discovery at La Venta of fragments of wood which were amenable to the radiocarbon technique. When these dates were published they proved a revelation, giving a time period for La Venta bracketed by 1154 and 604 BC. In one fell swoop the Maya protagonists and those who simply could not believe Stirling's reading of the Stela C inscription from Tres Zapotes had the ground cut away from under them. Even Stirling and his colleagues, who had championed the Olmec cause from the beginning, had to re-evaluate their ideas in the light of such early dates. It now seemed as though Olmec civilisation had been well under way by 1000 BC: in other words, it was some 3,000 years old and had been flourishing a millennium before the emergence of the Classic Maya.

As if his pioneering efforts at Tres Zapotes and La Venta were not spectacular enough, Stirling's unique blend of intuition and archaeological skill held fast for yet another great Olmec discovery. In 1945, along with his collaborator Phillip Drucker, he found the site of San Lorenzo, located on a tributary of the Coatzacoalcos river in the state of Veracruz. In fact San Lorenzo was not a single site but a grouping of three smaller sites—Tenochtitlán (not to be confused with the later imperial Aztec capital of the same name), Potrero Nuevo and San Lorenzo itself. This group yielded no less than five more colossal stone heads carved in the same fashion as those from La Venta and Tres Zapotes, and some 15 miscellaneous stone sculptures. San Lorenzo was the subject of more detailed investigations by the Yale archaeologist Michael Coe during the 1960s, and from these excavations came even earlier dates for the Olmec.

The Olmec had first appeared on an archaeological stage dominated by the much better known Maya civilisation; they had appeared as a mysterious and enigmatic people whose shadowy presence was felt and hinted at by the strange, beautifully carved jades, but whose body had remained incorporeal. As hint followed hint and artefact followed artefact, they emerged from the shadows to take centre stage as the earliest and most innovative of all Mexico's prehistoric civilisations. Even after Coe's detailed excavations at San Lorenzo, there were no identifiable predecessors.

In typically evocative style Covarrubius summed up the discoveries which led to the identification of the Olmec as Mexico's first civilisation. In his book *Mexico South*, published in 1946, he described the Olmec thus:

A great and mysterious race of artists seems to have lived since early times on the Isthmus, particularly around Los Tuxtlas and the Coatzacoalcos

Colossal Olmec head from San Lorenzo, discovered in 1945 by Matthew Stirling. *Photo, Author*

River Basin. Everywhere there are archaeological treasures that lie hidden in the jungles and under the rich soil of southern Veracruz, burial mounds and pyramids, masterfully carved colossal monuments of basalt, splendid statuettes of precious jade, and sensitively modelled figurines of clay, all of an unprecedented, high artistic quality. The tantalising presence of a great and remote past in what is now uninhabited, impenetrable jungle . . . [appeared] . . . suddenly out of nowhere in a state of full development, they constitute a culture that seems to have been the root, the mother culture from which later and better known cultures sprang.

This description was of course only an initial assessment and is couched in terms which stress romantic notions about the Olmec and the artistic side of their achievements. It does, however, capture the excitement which was felt in the early years of Olmec archaeology.

The Olmec had created Mexico's first true art style centred on the image of a feline, which appeared both naturalistically and transmuted into human form—caught as it were in the act of transformation—half-jaguar and half-human. Today the arguments which raged at the time, due to the early dates assigned to the Olmec, are largely forgotten, but the debate continues as to the nature of Olmec culture and the social and economic processes which led to its formation. The Olmec had made a spectacular entrance, but it was now time to examine them in depth, chronicle their achievements and place them firmly and securely within the overall picture of ancient Mexican civilisations.

CHAPTER 3

RECOVERING THE OLMEC CIVILISATION

The famous Mexican archaeologist Ignacio Bernal has referred to the swampy tropical forests of Veracruz in eastern Mexico as the 'metropolitan area' of Olmec civilisation, for it is here that all the great Olmec centres have been discovered. Covering some 18,000 square kilometres, most of this land is less than 100 metres above the sea level of the Gulf of Mexico. The entire region comprises the alluvial flood plains of the rivers Tonalá, Coatzacoalcos and Papaloapan, with only the volcanic Tuxtla mountains, rising like a series of natural pyramids to about 600 metres, breaking the monotony of the landscape. This low-lying, lagoon-ridden region endures no shortage of water, with two rainy seasons (June to November and January to February) easily replenishing the area's rivers, streams and swamps.

Due to annual flooding the soil along the river margins is extremely rich, with its fertility constantly renewed by the vast amounts of silt deposited in the wake of the seasonal rains. Such an area would seem to be ideal for manipulation by man in his efforts to grow crops on a large scale and on a regular basis. Unlike other parts of Mexico, the state of Veracruz has, if anything, too much rather than too little surface water. This is an important point to consider when we look at the Olmec gods whose counterparts in other regions of Mexico are usually referred to as rain gods. If, as some believe, the rain gods of Mexico originated with the Olmec, then there may be a fundamental difference here, inasmuch as Olmec gods were petitioned to 'control water' rather than simply 'send it'.

The Olmec region was therefore blessed with ample water for irrigation agriculture, and it also abounded in wild game—deer, tapirs, jaguars, waterfowl, monkeys and a variety of salt and freshwater fish and molluscs—all available in large quantities and doubtless used to supplement the Olmec diet. Indeed, some of these animals found their way into Olmec iconography— especially the largest of all American cats, the jaguar, whose natural domain includes such watery environments.

If the area was richly endowed with some of nature's most bountiful resources, this was partly offset by two serious drawbacks. Firstly, such necessities as hard stone for making *manos* and *metates* (for grinding maize), and the volcanic glass called obsidian, either did not occur locally or were not easily obtainable. Secondly, such an environment was not easy to tame: its marshy and riverine nature meant that it was difficult to plan and build ceremonial centres and even more difficult to locate and transport the large quantities of building stone that were necessary for monumental buildings and large-scale stone sculptures. The jungle itself, with its amazing regenerative powers, would only have added to these difficulties. Yet despite these considerations, the Olmec successfully came to terms with their environment, taking advantage of the long stretches of standing and moving water to overcome the logistical problems.

Quite apart from the environmental constraints, what can we say about Mexico's first civilisation? Ancient peoples were not mere machines striving for 'efficiency' in their daily struggle with nature—they did not necessarily seek a balance with their environment which would make sense to us. Often they worked within a different cultural framework, seeing the animals and landscapes around them not as 'objects', but rather as 'subjects'—living entities with a spiritual identity and life force of their own. The Amerindian world-view is, to Western ideas, a strange and foreign universe, but for the Indian it was dominated by powerful and ambivalent spirit-forces. Such a view naturally shaped their society and the monuments and ceremonial centres whose scattered remains are the archaeologist's domain. Whilst it is necessary to excavate and catalogue, it must always be borne in mind that, when we come to *interpret* the archaeological record, we must attempt to view it not from our perspective, but from theirs.

The Olmec of La Venta

Situated about 18 miles inland from the Gulf of Mexico, on an oval 'island' some four-and-a-half kilometres north–south and 1,200 metres wide, is La Venta, an archaeological site largely despoiled by the twentieth century's passion for energy. Today the area is controlled by PEMEX, the Mexican stateowned oil company, and most of its extraordinary stone sculptures have been removed to a specially built archaeological park in Villahermosa, capital of the adjacent state of Tabasco.

La Venta itself is dominated by its artificial volcano-shaped pyramid which still stands, even after the passage of nearly three millennia. In 1968 it was cleared of tropical vegetation and archaeologists realised that, unlike other Mexican pyramids, this earliest example had possessed neither a central stairway nor a shrine at its summit. It was estimated that its volume was about 99,000 cubic metres. For a variety of reasons, this first example of Mexican pyramid building has never been fully investigated, and so the tantalising possibility exists that, as with other similar but later structures, the La Venta pyramid may conceal an important burial or dedicatory cache.

Stretching northwards from the pyramids are two long, narrow mounds, with a smaller, circular mound just off centre; in front of this lies a ceremonial plaza which was originally surrounded by a row of two-metre high basalt

Model of pyramid and forecourt at La Venta *Photo, Author*

columns, each weighing some 700 kilograms. To the north of this is a large, terraced clay mound. Although no exact function for this elaborate complex has yet been identified, some authorities, perhaps fancifully, have seen in its overall design a giant stylised jaguar face. The whole area had evidently been carefully planned and laid out along an axis orientated some eight degrees west of true north.

Like San Lorenzo, the centre of La Venta must have been an impressive sight in its heyday. The earthen architecture, the stone sculptures and the clay floors were probably all brightly coloured with the varied hues of the rainbow. A contemporary observer standing on the pyramid would have looked out over a ceremonial centre dotted with colossal stone heads, free-standing sculptures and the famous if misnamed 'altars' with their decorative friezes showing episodes from Olmec mythology, in which the denizens of the jungle mingled with human beings in a fantastical array of supernatural representation.

Archaeologically La Venta is a mixed blessing for today's investigators; in the past, archaeologists spent most of their time and effort recovering concealed sculptures, surveying the size of the site and searching for 'monumental' evidence. Over the past three decades, however, anthropology has had a distinct impact on archaeology, and today's generation is more interested in reconstructing the processes of civilisation and tends to look for mundane everyday remains which might shed some light on how the Olmec went about their everyday lives. Whilst La Venta, with its wealth of stone sculptures, was a godsend to the former style of archaeological research, the wet and humid climate, combined with the acidic soil, means that there is a very poor preservation of such useful and datable materials as food remains and animal and human bones.

The La Venta Olmec had an intriguing practice of ritually burying precious materials in what are called dedicatory caches. No less than nineteen such deposits have been found in the area just to the north of the pyramid complex. Such offerings consisted of jade 'jaguar' maskettes, serpentine and jade axes, stone necklaces and a variety of earrings, pendants and the like. Often the quantity of such offerings from a single cache was enormous—in Offering No. 9, for instance, there were no less than 1,180 individual pieces.

Without doubt the single most extraordinary discovery, however, was made to the north-west of the ceremonial court. Here, Offering No. 4, buried under some 60 centimetres of soil, revealed a carefully arranged group of 16 delicately carved and finely polished Olmec figurines—two of jade, 13 of serpentine and, perhaps significantly, one of a red volcanic tuff. Behind this deliberately distinctive individual was a row of six jade celts (edged implements). All the figurines in this cache were typically Olmec in appearance, being depicted as asexual, with bald, mis-shapen heads, slanted eyes and the characteristic drooping mouth which has been called 'feline'. The weathered aspect of these beautiful but enigmatic objects suggests that they were already old when deposited and so were not made especially to be buried. A curious feature of this cache was what has been called a 'check-shaft', which had been dug directly over the centre of the cache, breaking through the multicoloured clays of the original burial. Apparently satisfied that the offering was still intact, the hole had then been filled up again during prehistoric times. All the objects buried in Offering No. 4 appear to have been originally painted red; we shall return again to this unique discovery when we attempt to recreate a picture of Olmec religious beliefs.

If the theme of the jaguar was slight in the statues of Offering No. 4, it was much more pronounced in another discovery—that of a mosaic of serpentine blocks enveloped in a layer of olive-coloured clay. Philip Drucker, Robert Heizer and Robert Squier, who excavated La Venta in 1955, described this extraordinary discovery thus:

> The mosaic represented a very highly conventionalised mask of the jaguar, and incorporated most of the distinctive features repeated in other Olmec representations of this deity . . . four diamond-shaped appendages on the south side represented either a headdress or plumes. Within the main square area of the mask the four small open spaces with castellated upper edges represented four eyes, with the plumed eyebrows of the typical Olmec Jaguar representation. The long narrow panel in the centre of the mask represented the nose, and the wide area across the lower portion, the mouth with lip and fangs,

Whilst some authorities do not necessarily accept this interpretation, it must be added that at its south-west corner was found a headless and kneeling human figure carved in basalt, with a circular concave pendant hanging as it were on the breast. This figure had its hands clasped as if in prayer, perhaps worshipping the possibly feline god whose gigantic face lay before it.

Beneath this mosaic was yet another layer of olive- and blue-coloured clays, and a set of rough, irregular chunks, mostly of serpentine, arranged in 28 levels. Drucker, Heizer and Squier labelled this discovery 'Massive Offering No. 1' and the area of its discovery as Feature A-1-e. They also made some preliminary calculations as to the human effort involved in its construction. They estimated the total volume of the deposit as some 20,500 cubic feet, of which some 13,650 cubic feet represented the stone objects alone! Even more remarkable was the fact that, when translated into weight, there were about 1,000 tons of stone in Feature A-1-e, all of which had had to be brought from a considerable distance. It is worth mentioning that this was not an isolated discovery: several other such massive offerings were also uncovered.

Further startling evidence on the nature of Olmec society came with the discovery of a giant burial known as 'Tomb A'. Lying just to the north of the pyramid, this tomb was built of basalt columns covered over with earth. As we have already seen, neither the soil nor the climate of the Olmec region are conducive to good preservation of such fragile faunal remains as human bone, but from the fragments which did survive it is thought that the tomb contained two small individuals, probably children. Both were apparently covered with red ochre and accompanied by luxury items for the afterlife, including a female figurine with a shining haematite mirror on her breast, and a shell-form jade pendant.

Monumental Tomb A from La Venta, made from basalt columns. *Photo, Author*

The highland 'Olmec' site of Chalcatzingo, Morelos. The ruins are scattered on level ground between the two peaks. *Photo, Author*

Seated Olmec ruler from La Venta. Note the elaborate headdress and the 'X', possibly denoting a mirror, displayed on the chest and stomach. *Photo, Tony Morrison, South American Pictures*

Olmec jade plaque. *Photo, Courtesy of the Trustees of the British Museum*

Olmec ceramic figurine of seated person – possibly a priest/ruler – wearing a jaguar or perhaps a cayman skin. From Atlihuayán, state of Morelos. *Photo, Author*

An Olmec 'altar' from La Venta. The central figure sits within a stylised jaguar mouth, which may represent an earth monster, whose eyes and fangs are prominent. Such 'altars' may have served as thrones for Olmec rulers. *Photo, Tony Morrison, South American Pictures*

In the same funerary vein was a stone sarcophagus adorned with a face of a feline monster; its interior was daubed with red ochre, and although the remains of the tomb's original occupier were all but non-existent, the burial yielded a serpentine figurine and several earrings as an indication of social status.

Perhaps one of the most distinctive aspects of La Venta's Olmec heritage was the group of monuments called, somewhat misleadingly, 'altars'. No less than seven of these carved monolithic blocks were uncovered, five of them depicting a seated figure emerging from a niche carved into one side of the block. Several of these 'altars' display this central seated figure holding a 'baby' in its protective arms. The 'baby' theme is most pronounced on altar No. 5, which has preserved not just the central infant cradled in the adult's lap but also four others, two on each of the lateral sides of the altar, and all held by an adult. The central niches have been interpreted as stylised jaguar-monster mouths which, in Olmec mythology, may have represented cave entrances into the under-world. The altars themselves may well have served as thrones upon which the ruler sat, surrounded by artistic representations of his mythological jaguar origins.

In addition to the altars, five carved stelae were found, all varying in the degree and sophistication of execution. Stela 1 depicts a standing Olmec figure wearing a helmet, earrings and a skirt, overlooked by what the French archaeologist Jacques Soustelle has called a stylised jaguar mask. Stelae nos. 2 and 3 are somewhat more elaborate in conception and execution. The former has a shortened figure with an elaborate three-level headdress surrounded by six smaller human figures, all of which are masked. The latter shows a meeting between two Olmec individuals, also surrounded by smaller figures.

La Venta had even more to offer: four colossal stone heads weighing between 11 and 24 tons each. These great basalt heads (there never were any accompanying bodies) are a unique aspect of Olmec monumental stone sculpture which have generated many flights of fantasy in their interpretation. Although the early explorers thought them 'negroid' in appearance they are in fact purely Mexican. Interestingly, they differ significantly in their execution from the other carvings found at La Venta, showing no sign of the stylised approach so prevalent elsewhere in Olmec sculpture—there are no feline attributes, no drooping mouths or cleft foreheads. These largest of all Olmec sculptures seemed to have represented actual people, individuals who were perhaps the rulers of La Venta. Whereas the repertoire of stylised sculptures conveys perhaps an 'ideological message' illustrating Olmec myth and belief, the stone heads offer us a limited but fascinating insight into the nature of the Olmec ruling dynasties. They provide us with perhaps the only accurate information we shall ever have as to what the Olmec actually looked like when stripped of their ubiquitous stylisation. They are at the same time monumental, enigmatic and intimidating, yet goad us with their apparent realism.

One of the most intriguing features of these colossal heads, and one which may support their interpretation as representations of actual historical rulers, is to be found in their 'American Footballer' style of headdress. Completely unlike the elaborate headgear found on the stelae, it is more akin to a skull cap, but each one is different, as are the respective ear ornaments. Each headdress possesses its own distinctive emblem which may prove to be individual 'name-glyphs' (so common amongst the later Maya), identifying for the Olmec—but, sadly, not for us—the names, lineage and status of the individual concerned.

Altogether some ninety stone sculptures have been found at La Venta, although doubtless many others remain to be excavated, and this sculptural tradition has given rise to a host of interpretations. Small standing statuettes, seated figures and fragments of larger, now lost statues have been discovered, one of the most provoking being that referred to as Monument 19, found in Complex A in 1944 by a Mexican oil worker. It is a block of basalt depicting an Olmec figure in profile and wearing a highly decorative headdress in the form of a jaguar mouth worn almost as a helmet. Ear-spools adorn the head and the whole figure has a large serpent curling up along the back, with its snarling face (capped with its own headgear) on top of the human figure. Many specialists have commented on this sculpture, some seeing in it the ancestor of the famed 'Plumed Serpent' or Quetzalcóatl, so prevalent in the art of the later Aztecs.

Archaeologists, of course, are interested not only in the description of a site and its cultural remains, but also in building a chronology for the people who constructed it. At La Venta the earliest phase seems to date from *c.* 1100–1000 BC, and it was then that work commenced on the ceremonial centre itself. During the second phase (1100–800 BC) the Olmec began burying their huge offerings in the rich tropical soil—covering them with layers of multicoloured clays and carrying out the ritual, presumably, amidst the panoply of religious and political ceremonial. Phases three and four span the years from 800 to 400 BC, and during this period the jade figurines and monumental tombs were made; at this time La Venta reached its height of political, religious and cultural prestige.

Somewhere between 450 and 325 BC La Venta went into a rapid decline—all building activity ceased as did the manufacture and interment of the jade figurines. Whatever the exact reasons for the marked decline of this remarkable centre, it is a fact that many of the monuments were deliberately defaced or destroyed.

The San Lorenzo Olmec

About 60 kilometres south-west of La Venta lies the equally impressive Olmec site of San Lorenzo. In reality, as we have already seen, this is a complex of small sites (Tenochtitlán, Potrero Nuevo and San Lorenzo itself) first discovered by Matthew Stirling in 1945. However, despite its alluvial floodplain setting, San Lorenzo differs in several important respects from La Venta. Whilst the latter has produced substantial evidence of massive offerings containing jadeite and serpentine, the former has yielded no such large scale dedicatory caches or tombs. In addition, La Venta possesses a far greater number of building platforms than does San Lorenzo, although it is the latter site which possesses a unique design in its overall layout. Significantly, whereas very little evidence of the debris of habitation has been found at La Venta, San Lorenzo has produced many examples of re-used domestic middens.

The plateau of San Lorenzo rises some 50 metres above the low-lying basin of the river Coatzacoalcos. This plateau is largely artificial and Michael Coe, who excavated the site during the mid 1960s, believes that its whole area was sculpted to represent a giant stylised bird of prey flying towards the east. However, he also notes that this huge undertaking was, for some unexplained reason, never completed. On the summit of the plateau, arranged along a north–south axis, is the main grouping of prehistoric mounds, small pyramidal structures and associated rectangular courtyards. Coe believes that one of these structures is Mexico's first ball-court, and indeed his investigations have yielded figurines which, in his opinion, represent ball-players.

Due to the meticulous excavations carried out by Coe and his co-worker Richard Diehl, we are able to say much more about San Lorenzo's cultural development, ceramic types and ecological base than the partial evidence from La Venta allowed; this is partially due to the different research objectives of modern archaeology which, as already noted, concerns itself more with 'culture process' than with simply retrieving monuments. Although the earliest traces of human activity at San Lorenzo appear about 1500 BC, it was not until some 300 years later, around 1200 BC, that the site took on a distinctly Olmec appearance. Again, as at La Venta, the many stone monuments were carved from the basalt quarries of Cerro Cintepec in the Tuxtla Mountains, some 70 kilometres away. The earliest Olmec phase at San Lorenzo produced eight magnificent colossal heads and examples of the so-called 'altars' weighing up to 40 metric tonnes.

One of the most fascinating archaeological features uncovered by the Yale expedition was an intact section of a 'drainage system' composed of small U-shaped basalt blocks, some of which still had their original capstones in place. Coe and his colleagues traced some 170 metres of this system in the south-western sector of the site. This hydraulic achievement apparently had nothing to do with either hygiene or agriculture, but seems to have been connected with the ritual water supply to a series of artificial 'ponds' dotted about the centre of the site. These stone-lined depressions have been interpreted as being associated with the worship of a rain god whose sacred rituals may have included bathing. Although the exact significance of such a complex system of water control is unknown, the 30 tons of basalt so far located represent a vast investment of time and effort.

One hitherto unsuspected discovery at San Lorenzo was evidence which implied that the Olmec inhabitants may have been cannibals—even if only on ritual and religious occasions. Burnt and broken bones were found in the deposits of domestic refuse or 'middens', although exactly who ate whom is a matter for grisly conjecture. However, the ceremonial eating of one's enemies, in order to acquire their physical strength or 'soul essence', is well known

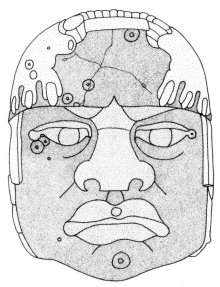

Monument 5 from San Lorenzo. Colossal Olmec head with two jaguar paws as part of the elaborate headdress. *Drawing, Pauline Stringfellow, after Coe and Diehl 1980, Fig. 428*

among many indigenous societies throughout Central and South America; the evidence for true cannibalism, that is, eating people for physical rather than spiritual sustenance, is more indistinct.

The painstaking excavations at San Lorenzo had, as one of their main objectives, the establishment of a reliable and secure chronology for the site itself. In order fully to understand what was going on and when, it was necessary to establish a series of identifiable phases allied to ceramic types and confirmed by stratigraphy and radiocarbon dates. The investigations defined five major cultural periods which span the years 1500–700 BC, the earliest period significantly preceding that of the first Olmec phase at La Venta.

The first two phases, 'Ojochi' and 'Bajío', apparently represent a non-Olmec occupation of the area. The third phase, known as 'Chicharras' (1250–1150 BC), saw the advent of a recognisable Olmec era during which typically Olmec artefacts and materials appear. Beautiful white kaolin figurines, kaolin pottery, a distinctive ceramic type known as 'Mojonera Black' and the beginnings of monumental stone carving all appear for the first time during this phase. These culture traits are almost completely new and possess few if any recognisable predecessors anywhere else in Mexico. This is one reason why the true origins of Olmec civilisation are so difficult to ascertain. Where did the Chicharras people come from? Did they develop from the earlier non-Olmec inhabitants or were they newcomers from outside?

It was also during the Chicharras period that the non-local raw materials, for

Olmec figurine of kaolin. *Photo, Author*

example, sandstone and obsidian, so important to the Olmec, first appeared at San Lorenzo. Their presence indicates effective methods of obtaining such materials from sources often several hundred kilometres beyond the Gulf Coast.

The fourth cultural period was labelled the 'San Lorenzo' phase (1150–900 BC); this era saw the site attain its zenith of political and religious power and also its greatest size. Two important types of pottery were identified and act as archaeological 'markers' for the period—'Calzadas Carved' and 'Límon Carved-Incised'. Significantly, both possess typically Olmec designs executed in relief on their surfaces. Of additional importance was the fact that these two distinctive pottery types appear in other parts of Mexico as well—the Valley of Oaxaca, the Valley of Mexico and at the unique highland site of Chalcatzingo. This widespread appearance of San Lorenzo-phase Olmec artefacts is especially intriguing as it contrasts sharply with the absence in the very same areas of pottery from the preceding Chicharras phase. The transition between the Chicharras and San Lorenzo phases seem to have marked a significant development in the nature of Olmec society, perhaps from a parochial culture to a civilisation with pan-Mexican influence.

The final phase of development with which we are directly concerned is called 'Nacaste', spanning the years between c. 900 and 700 BC and encompassing what could be termed the cataclysmic collapse of classic Olmec civilisation. The monumental heads, along with many other examples of Olmec stone sculpture, were deliberately defaced and purposefully buried in the rich soil of the site. At the same time new forms of pottery appeared, which seem to have no connection with preceding types. The 'Nacaste' phase probably represents some sort of violent upheaval in Olmec society accompanied by a presumed, but unproven, invasion of the area by non-Olmec peoples. It is possible, given the overlap in dates between San Lorenzo and La Venta, that some sections of San Lorenzo society left the site and settled at La Venta.

Other Olmec Centres

Although La Venta and San Lorenzo are by far the best known and most extensively investigated of the ancient Olmec sites, it would be a mistake to think that they were the only ones. Even today, large areas of the Gulf Coast are still relatively unknown archaeologically and remain difficult of access; many perhaps greater Olmec centres may still await discovery and the weaving of their individual site histories into the overall tapestry of Olmec civilisation. Some other Olmec sites have, however, been identified, although their full investigation awaits a future generation of archaeologists.

Nestling in the foothills of the volcanic Tuxtla mountains is the famous site of Tres Zapotes where some 50 mounds lie scattered over an area of about three kilometres. By comparison with La Venta and San Lorenzo, little is known about this important site, although it may have taken on the mantle of Olmec civilisation after the demise of the latter two centres, perhaps around 400 BC.

Tres Zapotes has been labelled 'Epi-Olmec', with an art style that shows signs of both pure Olmec and later styles. Indeed, from the deepest levels so far excavated typically Olmec ceramics have been retrieved, and of course the colossal stone heads found by Stirling are also characteristically Olmec. With its wealth of mounds, terraces and stairways, the site cries out for detailed investigation, for it must have been of great importance during the Olmec period. It is thought by some archaeologists that the earliest phase of occupation parallels the earliest phase at La Venta. Within a radius of some 25 kilometres of Tres Zapotes, no less than eight other sites have been identified.

Approximately 55 kilometres south-east of Tres Zapotes lies the site of Laguna de los Cerros which possesses some 95 mounds spread over 100 acres. One colossal Olmec head has so far been located, as well as a variety of stone sculptures in typically Olmec style. Laguna de los Cerros seems to have been occupied right down through the centuries of Mexican prehistory, from Olmec times to the Postclassic period which began around AD 900. Undoubtedly it was a major Olmec centre which may well predate La Venta and prove contemporary with the San Lorenzo phase at San Lorenzo. The already mentioned important pottery markers of Calzadas Carved and Límon-Carved-Incised have been found here and some authorities believe it may yet prove to be the earliest of all Olmec centres.

At the northern edge of the Olmec area lies the enigmatic site of Cerro de las Mesas, visited in 1927 by the famous Mayanist Herbert Spinden and archaeologically 'tested' by Matthew Stirling in 1941. The art style of the recovered artefacts appears to have more in common with the site of Izapa in the Mexican state of Chiapas than with classic Olmec civilisation; there are, however, traces of the Olmec at Cerro de las Mesas, not least those executed in bas-relief on Stelae 3, 4 and 9. Somewhat mysteriously, the site also boasts a colossal head standing some two metres high and yet fashioned in a style very different from those found at La Venta and San Lorenzo. If the inhabitants of Cerro de las Mesas are indeed later than the Olmec, were they perhaps consciously imitating them in the production of this giant head? Why this should be is still unknown. Despite the ambiguous status of Cerro de las Mesas, there is some evidence that the earliest levels of the site might yet yield purely Olmec occupation levels.

The Olmec Influence

The Olmec culture has an importance to Pre-Columbian Mexican civilisation far beyond that of its own existence. The new cultural ground which it broke and the social and technological processes it innovated had a profound cultural effect throughout ancient Mexico, both at the time and during later periods. It is because of this that the Olmec has been labelled the 'mother culture' of Mexican civilisation.

Whilst it was undoubtedly the humid tropical Gulf Coast states of Tabasco and Veracruz which were the Olmec heartland, other parts of Mexico also felt the precocious influence of this first civilisation. The volcanic central highland states of Morelos, Guerrero and Chiapas in Mexico, and the adjacent part of coastal Guatemala, have all yielded Olmec monuments or artefacts. The question which has vexed archaeologists for decades is the nature of this presence and the cultural effect of Olmec influence on less sophisticated peoples: was it military prowess, the result of proselytising Olmec priests (most of these monuments are decorated with powerfully dramatic 'religious' motifs), or was it purely an interest in economic extraction whereby the Gulf Coast Olmec acquired their raw materials?

Whilst the Olmec region possessed clay, haematite and basalt (the last from the Tuxtla mountains), fine stones such as serpentine, jade and schist, so important in Olmec ceremonial, are all metamorphic and had to be obtained from mountainous areas beyond the Olmec's swampy frontiers. The Olmec also made considerable use of magnetite and ilmenite, stones which could take a polish and were used as 'mirrors' in their ritual and regalia. The archaeologist Kent Flannery, who has occupied many years in excavating the Oaxaca valley, has suggested that this area produced the mirrors needed by the Olmec and perhaps traded them into the Gulf Coast on a commercial basis, receiving in return prestige items heavily imbued with Olmec ideology and decorated with Olmec motifs. Whilst there is evidence to support this argument from the early Oaxacan site of San José Mogote, it is nevertheless true that to date none of the mirrors found at San Lorenzo originated in the workshops of prehistoric Oaxaca.

Obsidian is another material of volcanic origin, which would have had to be brought in from outside the coastal area. The Olmec used a variety of obsidian types—each having its own geological source identifiable by various analytical techniques. Whilst many of these source areas have yet to be identified, the Olmec of San Lorenzo certainly made use of obsidian from both central Mexico and the highlands of Guatemala. One of their main source areas is known as 'Guadeloupe Victoria', located on the western flanks of the Pico de Orizaba, almost 100 kilometres west-north-west of San Lorenzo. Another important source lies 25 kilometres north-east of Guatemala City and is known as 'El Chayal', while others lie near to the central Valley of Mexico where they were used by the later metropolis of Teotihuacán. Undoubtedly there were well established obsidian trade routes in Mesoamerica from very early times and it is unlikely that, once these channels of communication had been forged, only material goods flowed along them—ideas, religious beliefs and ideologies probably went hand in hand with obsidian artefacts and luxury goods such as fine pottery wares, animal pelts and tropical foods.

It may have been a complex mixture of trade, reciprocal exchange of prestige items and even political marriage alliances which were the mechanism for spreading the Olmec influence beyond the Gulf Coast. However, in order to assess the importance of the Olmec for ancient Mexican prehistory, we must seek out these archaeological traces and try to place them in the overall context of this early period in Mexico's prehistory.

Olmec-style monuments and artefacts occur sporadically throughout Mexico, down through Guatemala into El Salvador, Honduras and possibly beyond to Costa Rica, where small Olmec-like jades have been discovered. Whereas such 'mobile' pieces could have been carried to these areas, some examples of Olmec influence are large, immovable rock carvings and stelae, which must have been hewn out of the living rock *in situ*. During the 1920s, at a site called Xoc on the edge of the Maya Lacandon jungle, a stone carving was discovered of a two-metre tall individual, executed in pure Olmec style on the face of a limestone rock. The figure had an elaborate headdress and was carrying a baton-like implement. Other similar monuments have been found in the mountainous state of Guerrero, and still others, like the impressive carvings at Pijijiapan on the Pacific coast of the Mexican state of Chiapas, are found scattered throughout south-western Mexico and the adjacent parts of Guatemala.

Although some of the smaller artefacts are undoubtedly 'heirloom pieces', passed on from one generation to another, the general evidence seems to argue for a piecemeal expansion by the Olmec for specific purposes to particular

Olmec polychrome mural from the cave sanctuary of Oxtotitlán, Guerrero. The personage is depicted wearing an eagle or eagle-jaguar skin, sitting on an altar whose decoration has features like a snarling feline. Note the 'banded-cross' eyes of the feline and the similarly rendered pectoral of the human figure, which may represent mirrors. *Drawing, Pauline Stringfellow, after Grove 1984, Fig. 39*

areas, rather than a blanket military conquest in search of an empire. Such an empire almost certainly never existed. One thing is certain, however: the nature of Olmec influence outside the heartland did not form an archaeological 'Horizon'—in other words, there was never a situation where identical cultural 'traits' occurred in widely separated areas in exactly the same context. Pieces of Olmec art and objects of material culture are usually intrusive and exist as but a small part of the total local assemblage of artefacts. The evidence from such 'Olmec' sites as Las Bocas, Tlatilco and Iglesia Vieja suggests that only about three per cent of the finds were Olmec inspired, perhaps representing special status or luxury goods. Many of the Olmec-influenced artefacts from the state of Puebla and the Valley of Mexico are white terracotta figurines and ceramics, portraying motifs such as the stylised jaguar faces and claws. Such materials have often been found accidentally, as at the burial site of Tlatilco, the site of Tlapacoya (which also yielded Olmec 'mirrors') and nearby Ayotla—all within the general area of the Valley of Mexico.

This evidence hardly concurs with notions of wholesale military conquest, the setting up of permanent Olmec colonies or the blanket imposition of Olmec rule. Such goods could have been traded into the area or 'bought' in exchange for the raw materials, such as serpentine and obsidian, which were used in abundance by Olmec craftsmen. There is also the possibility that a small number of Olmec controlled, to a greater or lesser degree, a local population which extracted these raw materials either directly or through inter-regional exchange with other peoples. Several of these isolated finds, however, may well prove to be part of an accompanying Olmec site when archaeologists get around to surveying and excavating the whole area of their discovery rather than merely recording individual carvings, stelae or jadeite and pottery artefacts. To date, only one such site, Chalcatzingo, has received detailed attention, and its investigation has revealed extraordinary facts about the Olmec presence beyond their Gulf Coast frontiers.

Chalcatzingo

Situated south of the Valley of Mexico in the rich agricultural state of Morelos, Chalcatzingo is without doubt one of the most spectacular of these Olmec-related sites or 'trading centres'. It is dominated by monumental stone sculpture, much of which is executed in a fashion strongly recalling the Olmec style, but simpler and more accessible, perhaps designed for a non-Olmec people who did not understand the byzantine complexities of a fully blown Olmec iconography; this feature is one of the major differences between the Olmec heartland and the so-called Olmec centres beyond the metropolitan boundary. As with other similar highland 'Olmec' sites, Chalcatzingo boasts a large number of non-Olmec artefacts manifestly rooted not in the Gulf Coast but in the Central Mexican tradition. The question naturally arises, what were the Olmec doing here?

The extensive archaeological evidence obtained by David Grove and his associates at Illinois University indicates that, as with San Lorenzo, Chalcatzingo had come into existence well before the arrival of Olmec influence. The site was strategically located in relation to natural vegetation zones and mineralogical deposits—especially the comparatively rare kaolinic clay which, when made into pottery, produced a white ceramic that is found throughout the Gulf Coast Olmec centres. Some authorities have suggested that Chalcatzingo was in fact a 'Gateway Community', with a redistributive role in such important materials as obsidian and the much prized greenstones which occur naturally in the neighbouring mountainous state of Guerrero. Chalcatzingo may have gathered up all the local raw material resources needed in the Olmec heartland and channelled them into this area. In return it received heavy Olmec influence which was reflected in its art style. From a geographic and cultural standpoint, Chalcatzingo was ideally situated between highland Central Mexico and the lowland Gulf Coast region—a strategically located half-way house.

By about 700 BC, according to this theory, there was a steady traffic in such exotic materials as obsidian from the Valley of Mexico, greenstone from Guerrero and kaolin from Chalcatzingo's own immediate hinterland. If this was indeed the case, a quasi-Olmec presence would have been required at the site and this may explain the impressive bas-reliefs carved into the rock face overlooking the settlement area. Might not a similar argument explain the appearance of other 'Olmec' sites scattered throughout Mesoamerica, such as Chalchuapa and Abaj Takalik in Guatemala? Did such an economic system play an integral role in the spreading of Olmec influence? We must also bear in mind the effect which this influence would have had on the recipient culture or settlement. Even if we discard ideas of military conquest, religious proselytisation and the establishment of colonies, the impact of the Olmec presence on culturally and technologically less sophisticated Mexican societies cannot be discounted.

Without doubt the major evidence for Olmec presence at Chalcatzingo are the large bas-reliefs mentioned above. Monument 1, known as 'El Rey' (the King), shows an important person, presumably a priest or chief, seated inside what has been variously interpreted as a cave or stylised jaguar mouth—the two being regarded as synonymous in later Mexican mythology. Above this figure are symbols representing clouds or rain; large volutes, or spirals, emerge from the mouth of the cave and possibly represent the rain-bringing breath of the jaguar god.

Monument 2 portrays three human figures standing over a seated and possibly bound individual—the former are all similarly dressed and carry clubs or paddle-like weapons, whereas the latter appears nude. The scene may represent a moment in an elaborate fertility ceremony. The sculptures at Chalcatzingo are alive with jaguar symbolism: Monument 4 depicts four figures, two human and two feline, and in both cases the feline is seen attacking the human figure which is reeling backwards under the force of the onslaught. Whilst neither of the human figures is decorated in any way, both felines

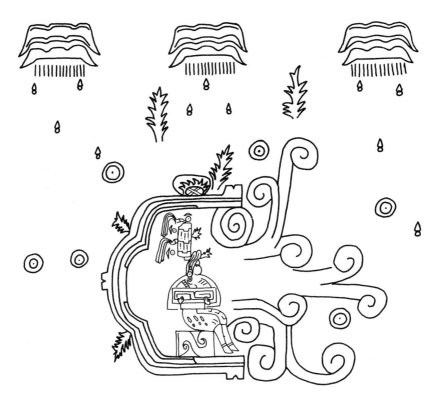

Monument 1 or 'El Rey' (the King) at Chalcatzingo, *Drawing, Pauline Stringfellow, after Grove 1984, Fig. 5*

possess either elaborate headgear or lines drawn on their torsos. Monument 3 portrays a naturalistic feline apparently in the act of licking the branch of a nearby plant; however, this monument is heavily damaged and a variety of interpretations have been put forward. All the sculptures at Chalcatzingo are dated to between 700 and 500 BC and belong to the 'Cantera' phase (as labelled by Grove)—these dates coinciding approximately with those from La Venta during its later period. Chalcatzingo itself was abandoned *c*. 500 BC.

The artistic conventions which link Chalcatzingo's sculptures to La Venta are also found in a distinctly different type of 'Olmec' site outside the Gulf Coast—the so-called 'painted caves'. The two most famous of these are Juxtlahuaca and Oxtotitlán, both hidden away in the mountains of Guerrero— the source of the greenstone deposits so valued in Olmec ceremonial life.

At Juxtlahauca, lying almost a mile inside a dark and labyrinthine cave, is the figure of a large Olmec figure drawn in profile and wearing a feathered headdress and jaguar skin. One wonders whether this represents merely a human wearing a jaguar skin or a half-human, half-jaguar creature from the nether world of Olmec mythology; elsewhere in the cave is a mural depicting a coloured jaguar facing a red snake.

The open cave-shelter site of Oxtotitlán is some 30 kilometres north of Juxtlahuaca's hidden murals, near the small and remote village of Acatlán where rites worshipping the jaguar are still enacted every May. At this site there are two significant paintings, both unfortunately very badly damaged by the passage of time. One shows a standing Olmec chief with elaborate headdress, raised arm and prominent phallus, facing a large jaguar. What can we make of such a scene? Was the Olmec figure copulating with the jaguar? Was the jaguar real or mythological? Or, perhaps, the Olmec chief's power, fertility and lineage were believed to emanate from an illustrious jaguar forebear? The second mural portrays an Olmec ruler seated on a throne that is itself a stylised jaguar-monster. This mural was originally a brightly coloured polychrome painting and it is probable that many of the personal adornments—here painted green—represented original artefacts of jade or greenstone. As already noted, the style of these cave paintings approximates to the style current at La Venta between 900 and 700 BC. What the Olmec were doing in these caves hundreds of kilometres from their Gulf Coast heartland remains a mystery.

Olmec archaeology has seen some of the most extraordinary developments in Mexican prehistory in recent years. The remains of this precocious civilisation, hardly known fifty years ago, are widely scattered all over Mesoamerica, from the tropical swamps of the Gulf Coast through the all but inaccessible sierras of Guerrero down to the Pacific coasts of the Mexican state of Chiapas and Guatemala. Isolated stone sculptures, sprawling ceremonial centres and a wealth of beautifully carved jadeite and serpentine figurines have all played their part in dragging Olmec civilisation from the shadows into the clear light of day. Given this vast amount of archaeological information, what can we now say about the Olmec themselves? What was their society really like, and what importance can be attached to their seeming fascination with a huge jaguar monster which dwelt in the dark recesses of caves and whose image adorns so much of their material culture?

CHAPTER 4

OLMEC ART, SOCIETY AND RELIGION

Incredible as it may seem, the 'cultural leap' forward which the Olmec achieved did not include the use of metals, either for sacred or secular purposes. Their civilisation was forged with a neolithic or stone-age technology and their great ceremonial centres, as well as their sophisticated art forms (regarded by many as the finest ever produced in ancient Mexico), were the result of stone on stone, human muscle and an intimate appreciation of the media with which their craftsmen worked.

What does this archaeological information tell us about the Olmec themselves? How did they live? What did they eat? What gods did they worship, and what was the relationship between religion and art? How *did* their society work? Was there perhaps a dynamic relationship between politics, ideology, art and the appearance of civilisation?

Olmec society, in common with most if not all ancient American civilisations, was in all probability based on tremendous inequalities which themselves may have been hereditary in nature. The vast amounts of organised labour and craft skills, whose silent testimony survives in the great monumental works of art, all indicate a tightly organised and well run society. As we have seen, the huge basalt heads, carved in what appear to be the likenesses of individuals, probably represented real people and embodied the power and majesty of Olmec kingship with its divine sanction. Such sculptures are a good indicator to the nature of their society; they are, however, only a part of the story.

If we are to flesh out the archaeological skeleton we need to turn to anthropology. Even so, such fundamentals as speech, music, songs, textiles, featherwork and a presumed wealth of wood carvings are all gone forever. The Gulf Coast environment was not an ideal location for preserving these delicate manifestations of human endeavour, and the once elaborate nature of Olmec ceremonial life died with the people themselves. Any attempt to reconstruct a fuller picture of everyday life around 1000 BC in the Olmec region is therefore hampered by many difficult problems.

Agriculture and Society

Great civilisations need a solid economic base upon which to build their own distinctive brand of culture, and the Olmec were no exception. Whilst some prehistoric peoples managed to create civilisations based on trade, warfare—and its corollary, tribute—almost all practised agriculture as well. The domestication of plants and, on occasion, animals, led to a way of life fundamentally different from that experienced by their hunting and gathering forebears. Lifestyles changed, populations tended to increase and people became jealous of the land itself. The transition from hunting to farming brought with it a massive leap forward in the way people thought about and organised their own society and in the way they regarded others. Agriculture, if practised intelligently and efficiently, could release a section of the community to assume new roles.

Examining the Olmec, there appears to be a link between a successful agricultural system and the emergence of a strong hereditary elite who, apart from claiming descent from powerful spirit-ancestors, also organised society on a day-to-day basis. This elite, in order to reinforce its authority, used people who were freed from the daily round of agricultural duties to specialise in a number of arts and crafts, to become priests, traders, textile workers and stone sculptors. Agriculture can therefore be seen as one key to understanding the precocious nature of Olmec society in its myriad aspects.

There are several types of agriculture which the Olmec could have practised, and although we cannot speak with certainty for a prehistoric society, we can make intelligent *guesses* based on modern practices both in the Olmec area itself and in other regions with similar environments.

Great strides have been made by archaeologists in recent years in assessing Pre-Columbian agricultural systems; most studies have dealt with the later Classic Maya civilisation, but, as the Maya were also a tropical rainforest people, some of the evidence may be appropriate to the Olmec also. The size of Olmec society and its evident sophistication argues strongly for a similarly effective agricultural system. 'Today', of course, is 'another time and place' and one must be wary of looking at what the modern inhabitants of Mexico's Gulf Coast do in terms of agriculture and then simply transferring this back into prehistoric times. Whilst the climate and geography of the Olmec heartland have not changed significantly in 3,000 years, the structure and motivations of society have. The form of a society is often a key to understanding how and why a particular culture developed a distinctive variety of agriculture. The needs of prehistoric Olmec centres and the shape of their society were not the same as the needs of the small scattered villages which dominate today's landscape. People must still eat, but contacts between different cultures, trade and politics often define how, when, and what they eat.

The basis of prehistoric Mexican agriculture was maize, and this was often grown alongside two other staples, beans and squash. This important triad is still found today at the site of Tres Zapotes and, indeed, in many other places throughout Mexico. In all probability the Olmec cultivated such plants as cotton, cacao, tobacco, tomatoes and chillis as well. Undoubtedly they also traded in other foods not native to their area.

By far the most prevalent form of agriculture found in Mexico today is that referred to by archaeologists and anthropologists alike as *swidden* or, more graphically, 'slash and burn'. In the Olmec region swidden agriculture involves the clearing of an area of jungle by cutting down the vegetation in March, and then burning it in the dry month of May. This process has the effect of enriching the soil with the resultant ashes, and in June, which marks the advent of the rainy season, the seeds are sown. The main crop, or *milpa del año*, is harvested between November and December, and in some cases, where a second crop (*tonamil*) is attempted, sowing takes place in January to be harvested the following June.

The problem with the swidden technique is that although a cleared field or system of fields can prove very productive at first, the soil soon loses its fertility, the plot has to be abandoned and new areas located and cleared. This type of agriculture is particularly wasteful of both human effort and available land; it also has the effect that human populations, in order to feed themselves, may have to split up and move off to other areas where new fields can be created. The swidden system would seem to act against political centralisation rather than encourage it. Since the nature of Olmec society reveals a strong sense of political centralisation and control, and although swidden probably played its part, another, more effective system must surely have dominated the agricultural landscape of the region during Olmec times.

It has long been recognised that civilisations arise in close relationship with their immediate environment, whatever course their culture subsequently takes. The Gulf Coast region is dominated by a number of rivers slowly winding their way across a flat and featureless landscape. Such an area is liable to periodic flooding as the result of tropical downpours so characteristic of the region. The question naturally arises, did the Olmec manipulate their environment and practise an efficient and extremely productive type of 'flood agriculture'?

Whilst many authorities have suggested this possibility, it was Michael Coe and Richard Diehl who, during their excavations at San Lorenzo in the mid-1960s, decided to explore the theory more fully and test it against current practices.

They found that the modern agricultural techniques around the Rio Chiquito were in fact far more sophisticated than the simple swidden method. The farmers of the area recognised four distinct agricultural seasons, during each of which they planted certain varieties of crops—the two major ones being called *tapachol* and *temporal* and the two lesser ones, *chamil* and *tonamil*. In addition there were two distinct techniques in use: a short-fallow swidden system on the higher land and, more significantly, a system of annual cropping along the flood banks of the River Coatzacoalcos.

The essence of Coe and Diehl's thesis in regard to the Olmec agricultural system is well summarised in their excavation report, *In the Land of the Olmec*:

Typical Andean scenery with valleys, snow-capped mountain peaks and cloud cover. *Photo, Author*

Stone Jaguar sculpture with Chavín-like features. From the highlands, possibly Pacopampa. *Photo, Author*

Carved stone head with prominent fangs and eyes, from Chavín. *Photo, Author*

The tropical rainforest of the Amazon. *Photo, Tony Morrison, South American Pictures*

Unique Olmec ceramic figurine from La Venta, showing a half-human, half-skeletal individual with typical Olmec features. *Photo, Author*

. . . the Olmec must have carried out a complex kind of agriculture in which maize and manioc were cultivated on two different kinds of soils. The first would have been the natural levees of the rivers, which are annually inundated by the summer rains; these could be planted only when the water level dropped, but the crops would have been in rich mud and silt. The second would have been the upland country around the San Lorenzo plateau; while the yields there would not have been so large, both a wet season and a dry season crop could have been harvested.

The Olmec seem therefore to have possessed an intimate knowledge of their surroundings and to have practised a type of agriculture which took ample advantage of local conditions, thus sowing the seeds of the hierarchical and kin-based social system that most archaeologists now agree led to the rise of their civilisation. It is tempting to suggest that certain families gained increasing control of the river levee lands and, utilising their above-average fertility, extended their holdings farther and farther; economic and consequently political power became concentrated in the hands of an elite, who subsequently manipulated this to their own advantage. Whilst it must be emphasised that this is but a theory, it certainly seems to fit in general terms the realities of the physical environment and the fact that we know through the archaeological record that the Olmec were a sophisticated society.

Quite apart from agriculture, on which the subsistence system was based, the Olmec also practised hunting within their immediate locality. The remains of animals they used for food reveal that about one third were terrestrial and the remainder aquatic—hardly surprising in such a riverine environment. A variety of turtles, ducks, toads and fish (especially the freshwater catfish and snook) were fundamental to their diet. Interestingly, dogs (ancient Mexico's only domesticated animal) formed about ten per cent of total vertebrate remains at San Lorenzo, and it appears that fishing and the hunting of estuarine waterfowl supplied the major part of their protein needs. Any family controlling the levee lands would thus be able to dominate the entire community.

A significant point is that the Olmec site of San Lorenzo probably emerged because the area in which it was located is not typical of the region in general. The San Lorenzo area contains much more fertile river levee land than the surrounding country. In a regional context, this area concentrates rich agricultural potential and, in the local context, the river levees represent the focus of potential economic and political power. Coe and Diehl themselves believe that the strategic siting of San Lorenzo will be repeated when similar studies are carried out at the locations of other major Olmec centres.

On the principle of inferring from the better known to the lesser known, archaeologists believe that they can propose explanations of prehistoric civilisations by reference to those which were seen by Europeans operating at the time of the Spanish conquest in 1519–21. We know that in ancient Mexico land belonged to kin groups rather than particular individuals. If we infer this later well documented reality back into Olmec times, we can suggest that the rich river levee lands belonged to Olmec kin groups, and that they could have used their pre-eminent economic power to weld together and support other smaller hamlets and towns, in such a way that a few Olmec groups would have exercised *de facto* political control over their entire surrounding area. Control of agricultural production and the means to redistribute it to others may have led to an increasingly centralised society.

If this hypothesis is anywhere near the truth, then such a concentrated form of economic power would also have been able to suck into the Olmec heartland such necessary raw materials as obsidian for tools and weapons. Olmec rulers could have controlled the harvest produced by their rich levee soils, organised their society and superintended 'export' of any surplus to the highlands— which, in return, sent raw materials not available in the Olmec region. In the guise of elaborate festivals and ceremonies, marriage and political alliances could have been sealed with gifts of essential raw materials, all having the sanction of the Olmec gods and spirits. Apart from the obvious benefit to Olmec society in general, such practices would also have reinforced the hold on Olmec society exercised by their ruling dynasties.

Controlling a society's basic needs meant that any ruling elite could have extended its economic and religious control in order to organise, plan and build elaborate ceremonial centres which would have served as an impressive and concrete manifestation of its natural and supernatural power. The appearance of large sculptures and architecture would have added to the prestige and mystique of the elite who may have invented a complete mythology to integrate economic power into the religious sphere.

Olmec Religion

Leaders of traditional Amerindian societies were—and in some remote areas still are—believed to possess special access to supernatural beings who, they considered, controlled everyday life. This point is especially pertinent when trying to understand Olmec religion, since this civilisation originated in a cultural milieu which had as much in common with what had gone before as with what came afterwards. In other words, we can perhaps carefully apply the ideas of present-day Amazonian societies in attempting to investigate the nature of prehistoric Olmec religion.

Whereas Amazonian societies have their sorcerers or shamans, the Olmec, being more numerous and more sophisticated than simple forest villages, would have possessed a hierarchy of priests or priest/chiefs and an organised pantheon of deities. These chiefs may have been the individuals whose likenesses were carved in the colossal basalt heads already described.

Assessing the nature of Olmec religion and ideology is one of the most difficult problems faced by archaeologists. By virtue of being Mexico's first civilisation, there were no pre-existing sophisticated cultures from which the

Olmec could borrow. Everything had to be invented or elaborated using time-honoured traditions of religious belief, and it is here that 'ethnographic analogy' is particularly useful. The Olmec were a pristine, not a secondary or imitative, civilisation. They invented, innovated and elaborated the basic religious and political system whose tenets can be traced down through the centuries, guiding a great diversity of later peoples.

The Olmecs created a new religious system, transferring and transmuting ancient hunting and gathering beliefs into stone, jade and pottery. For the first time they made mythology and religious belief tangible, visible and permanent. From the smallest jade carving to the most impressive mythically inspired stone sculpture, they used the skill of the artisan to convey a startlingly vivid impression, a vision of Olmec presence and power. The pre-eminence of the ruling elite, the tight control of society and the grandeur of Olmec civilisation itself was inextricably linked to the emergence of stone and jade images which conveyed the power of ancestors, human–animal beings and the control of cosmic myth and natural forces exercised by the rulers themselves.

The rich and sophisticated system of Olmec religious beliefs is only now being fully realised and, although opinions vary, it is the jaguar which seems to have played a central role. This is not to say that the imagery surrounding this powerful feline is the only major theme in Olmec iconography—this is certainly not the case—but it does appear to have played a dominant role.

To some extent, all religious power is grounded in the myths which reinforce and give sacred meaning to the rituals and ceremonies punctuating social life. Such rituals provide a structure within which a culture's view of its place in the universe, and its individual identity, are publicly stated and reinforced. All societies must have a similar mechanism by which they create and maintain social order.

In large, sophisticated civilisations, economic and political power is increasingly vested in the few, i.e. the elite, and is perceived to emanate not from the democratic process, but from the supernatural support of ancestors, gods and spirits. In other words, Olmec rulers were at pains to stress their connections with the supernatural and their access to and affinity with the omnipotent inhabitants of this other world.

One observable result of this connection between men and gods was the stress laid on the relationship of the ruling dynasties with animals which were believed to be large, successful and fierce, and thus charged with the raw power of supernature. The jaguar, as America's largest and most successful predator, was the ideal choice for this mystical identification with the elite.

Whereas in the early years of Olmec archaeology it was thought that all important Olmec art was inspired by the jaguar, today it is realised that this was not the case: serpents, birds, caymans and even spiders are all represented in a complex diversity of iconographic images. Whilst such animals were doubtless important to Olmec religion, it was still the feline which was portrayed as the dominant icon. Even today in Amazonian societies the jaguar is regarded as the 'Master of Animals', and is often described and portrayed as a central image around which other lesser animals, such as snakes and eagles, are clustered.

Nowhere is this relationship between the Olmec elite and the jaguar better seen than in the shattered remains of Monument no. 3, from Potrero Nuevo at San Lorenzo. The remaining base of this monument presents us with an image in stone which could have come directly from contemporary Amazonian Indian myth, for it represents a huge jaguar monster in the act of copulation with a supine human female. Many Amerindian myths abound with the imagery of such an event which created a race of part-human, part-jaguar beings—a story which facilitated the shaman's identification with this power-

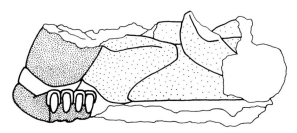

Monument 3 from Potrero Nuevo, San Lorenzo. Although heavily damaged, it appears to portray a huge jaguar being copulating with a supine female. Myths concerning the origins of 'jaguar people' through such a union are widespread in Central and especially South America. *Drawing, Pauline Stringfellow, after Coe and Diehl 1980, Fig. 497*

ful feline. In simpler societies it was the shaman who was identified with the jaguar, but in the complexity of Olmec civilisation the elite may have assumed this role, leaving the ritual and ceremonial duties to a full-time priesthood. As much of Olmec art contains an ideological message, we can perhaps suggest that the variety of feline symbolism within it serves to stress this mythological and mystical relationship between the jaguar and the ruling class.

Olmec art is full of complex symbolism which represented ideas and values prevalent in their society. Sometimes motifs were isolated from their original context and used as a kind of shorthand for fuller and more complex representations—such motifs include the so-called 'knuckle-dusters', 'torches' and the dramatic 'jaguar-paw-wing'. Whilst the message of Olmec iconography was ideological and these individual motifs were used to convey ideas, the Olmec did not possess writing in the true sense of the word.

Throughout many myths and beliefs held by a diversity of modern Amerindian societies, the jaguar is intimately associated with the concept of rain and fertility. Few scholars have asked why this should be so and have taken it on trust from other authorities. The reason for this association is in part biological and in part cultural. Throughout Central and South America, jaguars prefer to live near to watery environments, since the myriad rivers, lakes and water-logged savannahs offer a rich diversity of prey. Unlike many large cats, the jaguar has no aversion to water, often hunting by the river's edge and ever ready to take to water in order to attack fish, caymans and, on occasion, man. Indeed, there are stories of jaguars attacking Indians in their canoes.

Thus we have a complicated but fascinating link between nature and culture. The Olmec heartland must have been a favoured habitat for jaguars; the control of water, so necessary for river levee agriculture, was therefore associated with a large spotted cat whose natural domain was a riverine environment. This reality was grafted onto age-old shamanistic beliefs about the jaguar and what emerged was a new hybrid—a fully-fledged religion based in part on traditional beliefs but firmly locked into the new era, in which the 'control' of water was of paramount importance to the success of the new agricultural system upon which Olmec civilisation depended.

Olmec rulers may therefore have linked the realities of water control with a system of belief which identified prominent persons with prominent animals— the jaguar fulfilled all these needs. As the fertility of the soil depended on the annual rains and the identity and survival of the Olmec depended on successful agriculture, the complex strands of 'reality' became inextricably interwoven with myth. Such myths extolled the connections between the rulers and the supernatural animal *par excellence*—the jaguar. Thus it was the Olmec rulers who, by their affinity and supernatural links with the jaguar, could control the rains, the flooding which came in their wake and ultimately the vital food supply. It is within this context that we should perhaps evaluate the many general and specific images of the feline which appear so frequently in Olmec art and which speak so suggestively of Olmec religion.

Monument 52 at San Lorenzo was discovered in 1968. Made of basalt, it represents a seated half-human, half-feline figure some 90 centimetres tall, with a snarling 'were-jaguar' mouth, its paws resting on its knees. Michael Coe regards this figure as the Olmec rain god. Significantly, it was found at the head of the line of drains he uncovered and may perhaps be regarded as the guardian of the drainage system. As we have previously seen, this drainage system and the series of stone-lined ponds with which it was linked were probably for a religious rather than a secular use. The ritual control of water and feline symbolism—here we have a firm hint of the very nature of Olmec society.

Feline symbolism in Olmec art, whether naturalistic, stylised or anthropomorphised, is widespread: it may be depicted in small jadeite votive axes such as that in the British Museum and the Kunz axe, or in the large stone sculptures which are displayed either in Mexico's museums or *in situ*, in their original archaeological setting.

The jaguar was also a point of departure for more complex artistic forms, encoding, in all probability, a more elaborate set of religious ideas. The Olmec, like the Amazonian societies of today, rarely took the image of the jaguar, or any other animal, directly from nature but rather altered and transmuted certain features to create a distinctive and culturally defined 'ideal'. We are thus presented with individual characteristics of the jaguar taken out of context and re-combined to form something totally new, a fantastical creature which prowled the jungles of the mind rather than those of the tropical rainforest.

Birds have always had a distinctive symbolism all their own. They have feathers, wings and claws and can break the bonds of earth in skyward flight; they symbolise the ecstatic airborne sojourn of the human soul and can aid the shaman in his celestial voyages to speak to the spirits. Thus bird feathers and claws can be linked to human and feline characteristics to create another new 'creature', and this was done many times by Olmec craftsmen. Indeed, the Bororo tribe of central Brazil equate the beak and claws of the harpy eagle with the fangs and claws of the jaguar. Olmec art is full of such composite creatures. Together with the serpent, the feline characteristics of the Olmec period may mark the origin of the later and widespread belief in the 'Feathered Serpent' or Quetzalcóatl. This deity is well known from the much later Aztec civilisation, although a close inspection of this mythical 'creature' reveals a possible mis-identification.

Whilst Quetzalcóatl is often referred to as the feathered serpent (i.e. a composite bird-snake), a closer examination reveals that it may in fact be a mixture of three separate animals—with a jaguar's face and fangs, a serpent's body, and a bird's feathers. If this is so, then the complex of Quetzalcóatl features and their attendant beliefs may have originated with the Olmec. The famous stone sarcophagus at La Venta depicts what may be the original Quetzalcóatl figure. It is long, like the body of a serpent, and possesses a snarling feline face which itself is composite, due to its feathered eyebrows and distinctively serpent bifid tongue.

An intriguing number of serpentine figurines have been found, which seem to portray the jaguar as a man. Amazonian shamans claim to be able to turn into

Were-jaguar figurine of serpentine. There are paw-prints on the bottoms of the feet, traces of red pigment on the body, and the fists are drilled to hold something. Height 8 cms. *Photo, Courtesy of Dumbarton Oaks Research Library and Collections, Washington, D.C.*

Were-jaguar figurine of serpentine with pyrite eye inlay and snarling feline face. Possibly representing a masked dancer or a shaman transforming into a jaguar. Height 18.8 cms. *Photo, Courtesy of Dumbarton Oaks Research Library and Collections, Washington, D.C.*

this powerful cat to further their supernatural purposes. Whilst in contemporary Amazonian societies such claims are purely verbal, in Olmec times the idea of transformation was translated into solid form. In the Dumbarton Oaks collection in Washington there are several figurines which depict anthropomorphic felines, or man-jaguars. One is an eight-centimetre high statuette which has the head, feet and tail of a jaguar but the torso, arms and clenched fists of a human. Another piece portrays, in similar stance, a human body with a heavily felinised face—caught as it were in the act of transformation. There are several other similar pieces scattered throughout museums and private collections in Mexico and the USA. What are we to make of such enigmatic pieces of Olmec art?

Many interpretations have sought to explain these figurines. Did they portray actual individuals changing from man to animal, the idealised concept of man–animal transformation, or do they suggest that in an Amerindian world alive with 'spirit-force', everyone possesses a little bit of 'jaguar essence'? What is certain is that they represent the work of master-craftsmen in a sacred medium (serpentine), and that they were used in sacred or ritual circumstances. As such they presumably convey, as do the multitude of larger stone sculptures, a belief in a transformational universe where prominent people derive their power from access to prominent spirits, the most prominent and powerful appearing to have been the jaguar.

Evidence supporting the view that the jaguar was intimately connected with the Olmec dynasties lies in the art itself. As already mentioned, very few naturalistic felines are portrayed in Olmec art—they are most often shown with cultural elaborations, for example, humanised and wearing headdresses. At the highland 'gateway community' of Chalcatzingo, Monument 4 shows two felines attacking two humans who are falling backwards under the onslaught. These felines each possess extra, non-biological attributes. Whilst both have been interpreted as supernatural, the upper is rampant and much larger than the smaller, less active one. Both have their claws extended and both seem to be wearing headdresses of a kind. They may be variously interpreted as the Olmec conquest of highland peoples, the mythical dominance of Olmec deities over humans, or they may signify life and death, day and night, or perhaps the duality of male and female. What is certain is that the natural attributes of the jaguar are important as the symbol of superiority, dominance, ferocity and right to rule which was so fundamental to Olmec ideology. A mixture of biology and culture led to the creation of an art form which dramatically expressed Olmec ideals.

One particularly intriguing feline figure at Chalcatzingo is Monument 3 (already mentioned on p. 60) which portrays a naturalistic feline, apparently licking the branch of a large plant or tree. Whilst some have interpreted this as evidence for supernatural jaguars eating hallucinogenic plants, it may prove significant that the 'branch' being licked by the feline does not possess the characteristic circle-tip of the others: it may in fact represent an outstretched human arm with the accompanying head resting at the base of the tree or bush.

Monument 4 from Chalcatzingo, showing two stylised felines with elaborate headgear attacking two human figures, each of whom has the typically deformed Olmec head. *Drawing, Pauline Stringfellow, after Grove 1984, Fig. 30*

Unfortunately damage to the sculpture has precluded archaeologists from proving or disproving this most interesting idea.

There are, then, many examples of feline symbolism in the art of the Olmec. Very few are naturalistic and most have been altered to express an Olmec feline concept. In the painted caves of Guerrero, Olmec personages stand next to jaguars or sit on stylised jaguar thrones—images which imitate in polychrome mural the thrones, usually referred to as altars, carved in solid stone in the Gulf Coast heartland. Monumental stone sculpture, small scale carvings, cave paintings and rock sculpture all show, to a greater or lesser degree, the heavy influence of the jaguar. It is clear that what we are seeing is indicative of a complex and not fully understood Olmec religion; we are emphatically not witnessing a simple worship of jaguars, but a more involved belief in the supernatural qualities of the ruling dynasties which have associated themselves with what we have decided to call the jaguar deity, spirit or 'essence'. Olmec art displays the ideological message of Olmec religion; the concept of 'jaguarness', even if represented only by the addition of sharp teeth, fangs or snarling mouth, is ever present.

Natural jaguars provided the raw material for the Olmec in their thoughts about the cosmos and their place within it. Concepts of superiority, success, water control and access to the spirit realm were built up according to

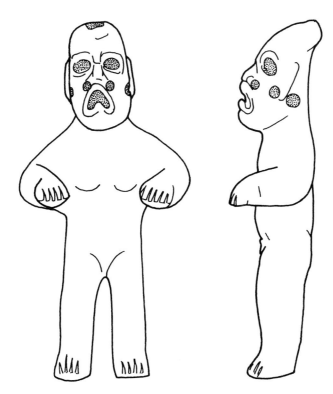

Olmec were-jaguar jadeite figurines showing typical features of misshapen head, snarling mouth and hands that could be paws. *Drawing, Pauline Stringfellow, after Grove 1984, Fig. 19*

characteristically Amerindian ideas about the nature of the universe. Such ideas are totally alien to us, but the use of feline imagery, so prevalent in the modern societies of Amazonia, is reflected in the archaeological record of Olmec times. What man did with the raw material provided for him by 'nature' depended on the culture itself. If the feline is dominant in Olmec religion it is because the Olmec themselves equated their position in human society with that of jaguars in the natural world. Jaguars are the 'Masters of Animals' and the Olmec regarded themselves as 'Masters of the Civilised World'. Once the jaguar had been chosen to express such ideals, it was only a short step to elaborating this theme and adding other attributes to fit the natural animal into a cultural framework.

Ancient Mexico's first art style was a product of its first true civilisation; the artistic content was an ideological message, and this message equated the supreme predator of the jungle with the supreme expression of culture. The Olmec were the most powerful cultural force in Mexico *c.* 1000 BC, and their political power, ceremonial centres and art forms all conveyed a pervasive ideological message. In such terms the Olmec were perhaps the People of the Jaguar.

CHAPTER 5

THE DISCOVERY AND ARCHAEOLOGY OF THE CHAVÍN CIVILISATION

In 1919 Julio Tello, widely regarded as the father of Peruvian archaeology, was exploring the spectacular Andean scenery of northern Peru. In the basin of the Pukcha river, in what today is a remote backwater in the department of Ancash, he discovered an impressive stone-built temple-pyramid—evidence of a previously unknown yet obviously sophisticated civilisation. Investigating further, he uncovered a startling array of carved stone monuments depicting, in a highly distinctive style, felines, serpents, human heads, caymans, lizards, raptorial birds and strange half-human, half-animal creatures. These designs, repeated on carved stelae, monolithic slabs and a variety of pottery and bone remains, indicated a high level of technological achievement and social organisation; the motifs themselves spoke of an ancient and mysterious prehistoric religion.

This remarkable archaeological site took the name of the small village on whose fringes it was located—Chavín de Huántar. Tello's discoveries were to have a profound effect on the development of Peruvian archaeology, initiating a debate on the nature and origins of ancient Peruvian society, which raged for many years and is only now beginning to fade. They also fuelled speculation about an ancient religious cult seemingly centred on a fierce feline deity.

Later that same year, Tello recognised motifs similar to those he had encountered at Chavín on the beautiful pottery and enigmatic goldwork displayed in museums throughout Peru. A gold plate and jug in collections at Trujillo, on Peru's north coast; a jug from Cajamarquilla in the department of Ancash; another in the San Carlos University museum and, significantly, Chavín-like motifs repeated on a number of gold ornaments from Chongoyape in the Lambayeque valley, again on Peru's north coast. Tello realised that although he had discovered at Chavín what was arguably the original source of a highly distinctive art style, many similar artefacts had been previously recovered and displayed, without anyone realising their full significance.

In the years that followed, Tello found intriguing evidence of Chavín artistic influence throughout the diverse regions of Peru, but these were often modified by local artistic traditions. One famous discovery was made in 1925 in the burial caves of Cerro Colorado, where the arid Paracas peninsula juts out into the Pacific from Peru's south coast. Here he found pottery covered with

Stirrup-spout bottle showing Chavín-like feline with spots and fangs. Of the type known as Tembladera from north coast of Peru. *Photo, Courtesy of the Trustees of the British Museum*

polychrome decoration, including motifs executed in the same style as those from Chavín—they were, however, tempered by additional features characteristic of the later Nazca culture further to the south. In the period 1926–7, pottery from the coastal midden sites of Ancón and Supe, which had previously been ascribed to a primitive culture of cannibal fishermen, were recognised by Tello as typically Chavín in their shape and decoration. Fragments of carved bone, gourd and textile, also from these two sites, suggested Chavín influence.

At this early stage all Tello had to go on was the repertoire of superbly carved stone sculptures and a number of pottery sherds at the site of Chavín de Huántar, a widely scattered collection of pottery from all over Peru, and some splendid gold artefacts from the North coast—all sharing motifs which he ascribed to Chavín. There was as yet no concept of a Chavín culture as such, nor any appreciation of the role which Chavín had played in the dispersal of its distinctive artistic motifs; and whilst the motifs spoke convincingly of the sophistication of their parent culture, neither Tello nor his colleagues could yet understand their 'language'.

Even before his discoveries at Chavín de Huántar, Tello's status was such that few argued against his interpretation of the finds. Consequently, in his subsequent investigations, whenever he reported Chavín-like art either in the high sierra or, more frequently, in the oasis-like river valleys which cut across the coastal desert, his interpretations were generally accepted. Then in 1933 he discovered what he called two splendid examples of Chavín art at the temples of Cerro Blanco and Punkurí in the coastal Nepeña valley. In the lower levels at both sites were the remains of impressive painted mud sculptures recalling the style and motifs at Chavín. At Punkurí he reported a spectacular feline head and paws, modelled in stone and mud and set at the base of a central stairway. Characteristically, these finds were interpreted as evidence for the Chavín culture's adaptation to a coastal environment. The often confusing and disparate evidence of Peru's prehistory was being fitted into a framework which had Chavín de Huántar as its inspiration.

Such influences were not confined to the desert coastline. Two years later, in October 1935, Tello spent a few days in the small village of Pukara near the northern shore of Lake Titicaca. Famous at that time for its earthenware pottery, the area also abounded with stone sculptures which, according to Tello, were dressed, polished and carved with figures similar to those from Chavín. Tello considered that Pukara's stone sculptures and pottery, both heavily imbued with feline imagery, showed definite signs of Chavín influence.

In 1937, whilst working for San Marcos University in Lima, Tello, accompanied by another respected Peruvian archaeologist, Toribio Mejía Xesspe, explored the Casma valley north of Lima as part of a brief which required him to search northern Peru for the oldest civilisations he could find.

Lying at the foot of a rocky outcrop known locally as 'Cerro Sechín', some seven kilometres east of the coastal town of Casma, Tello spotted the tops of five stone slabs emerging from the sandy surface. On investigating, he uncovered a whole series of slabs, decorated with gruesome faces and figures. One of these he described as a half-human, half-feline monster which, due to its distinctly unfriendly appearance, local inhabitants called the 'Huaca of the Fierce Idol'. Further excavation revealed three more carved blocks, depicting similarly grotesque human heads in profile. All were set up in a great platform—part of an ancient ceremonial centre. Altogether Tello found some 96 monoliths at Cerro Sechín, all executed in an apparently similar style.

Carved monolith from Cerro Sechín, on the Peruvian coast, showing warrior with a war-club. *Drawing, Pauline Stringfellow, after Roe 1974. Fig. 29a*

Despite having been encased in sand for untold centuries, these great carved monoliths nevertheless showed signs of a lengthy exposure to the elements, exhibiting a yellow patina over their exposed surfaces. They depicted full-length human figures, human torsos severed at the waist and isolated pieces of human anatomy including heads, eyes, possible vertebrae, intestines, bones, hands and feet. Such a gruesome collection of images has been variously interpreted as evidence for prehistoric surgery and for human sacrifice. The latter is the most likely explanation, as the segments of human bodies were set between elaborately dressed individuals marching towards a central stairway. Mass human sacrifice in a ritual context is clearly hinted at in what may be a macabre portrayal of power.

Whilst none of the slabs depicted anything remotely feline, and the engraving technique was markedly inferior to the monoliths at Chavín, Tello nevertheless suggested that they represented a later, degenerate imitation of the sophisticated Chavín carvings—sub-Chavín was his description. The suggestion that Cerro Sechín might predate Chavín de Huántar he dismissed out of hand, even though other eminent archaeologists acknowledged it as a distinct possibility.

In Tello's view, all this disparate evidence was conclusive: Chavín had emerged as Peru's pristine megalithic culture with its most important centre at Chavín de Huántar in the upper Marañon drainage in the Andes of north-central Peru. In ancient times, he believed, this culture had spread its influence outwards in all directions. Everywhere one looked there was some object, large or small, which recalled its distinctive style.

Stone sculpture, pottery, goldwork and monumental stone architecture all had Chavín as their inspiration, regardless of whether they were of typical classic Chavín appearance. The depiction of felines, monsters, birds, fish, snakes and half-human, half-feline creatures became a mark of Chavín influence. For Tello this influence was to be found throughout Peru, and even local traditions and developments were regarded not as independent cultural inventions, but as either local variations of Chavín or later degenerate and imitative versions. Thus Chavín became the prime example of Peruvian civilisation from which all subsequent cultures had developed—a veritable 'mother culture'—in much the same way that Olmec civilisation would be regarded a decade or so later in Mexico. Tello became convinced that Chavín occupation levels were the earliest evidence of civilised life in Peru, and his position as doyen of Peruvian archaeologists all but guaranteed that his views would become the orthodoxy of the day.

Although Tello emerged as the main proponent of Chavín as the base for all Peruvian civilised cultures, it was the German explorer Middendorf who, in 1894, had first suggested that Chavín was the capital of a pan-Peruvian coastal and Andean empire. Tello believed that Amazonian influences were great at Chavín and that the site's influences in turn extended over the Andes to Ecuador in the north and Argentina in the south. He saw the later coastal civilisations of the Mochica and Chimú as being inspired by the priests and mastercraftsmen of Chavín de Huántar, and regarded Chavín civilisation as the roots and trunk of a great 'cultural tree', whose branches were represented by the later, post-Chavín cultures.

The feline deity, so graphically depicted in the art of Chavín de Huántar, was seen as the unifying force in Andean culture. The Chavín phenomenon represented the history of the cultural development, elaboration and spread of this powerful deity and the rituals and symbolism which surrounded it. Tello set out these beliefs in his great work *Wira Kocha*, published in 1923. There is, of course, a great difference between what can be termed the Chavín Horizon, the Chavín Tradition and the Chavín Style. Whilst the notion of a 'horizon' concerned itself with chronology and the dates which bracketed the Chavín culture itself, the Chavín 'style' dealt with the way in which felines and other animals were technically and stylistically represented. The concept of a Chavín 'tradition' was simply concerned with the content of that style, that is, the predominance of feline, human-feline and animal representations. As we have seen, the latter are found in many Peruvian cultures which have nothing to do with the site of Chavín de Huántar, its lifespan or the highly distinctive style affected by its craftsmen. For Tello, the mere presence of feline symbolism indicated that the culture was an integral part of the Chavín tradition.

The whole issue of the existence and significance of Chavín de Huántar and its impressive array of artistic images and monumental architecture was not immune from the domestic politics of the day. Tello himself came from the highlands or *montaña*, and interpreted the existence of Chavín de Huántar and its great art style as proof positive of the Andean source of Peruvian civilisation. That other great Peruvianist, Rafael Larco Hoyle, took issue with this inter-pretation and suggested instead that Chavín was a coastal civilisation which had been taken into the highlands by pilgrims from the great coastal sites,

Carved jaguar sculpture from Chavín de Huántar, showing pelt markings, upward looking eyes, fangs and claws. *Drawing, Pauline Stringfellow, after Roe 1978, Fig. 1c*

especially those of the Nepeña valley. Significantly, he was a member of the land-owning class whose economic and political base was the coastal as opposed to the Andean region of Peru.

Larco's own ideas sprang from his discoveries, during the 1930s, of Chavín-like pottery at Cupisnique in the Chicama valley on Peru's north coast. His re-interpretation of Tello's coastal evidence saw the origins of the feline cult as residing not in the highlands but on the coast, and he saw Chavín de Huántar itself merely as a later colony founded by coastal peoples. He set out his beliefs in his important work, *Los Cupisniques*, published in 1941.

Chavín de Huántar: Archaeology of a Cult Centre

Spectacularly sited amongst the high snow-capped Andes of northern Peru, the site of Chavín de Huántar lies strategically placed within an easily defensible narrow river valley. Suitably located to both receive and distribute cultural influences, its position would have enabled it to filter and distribute material goods and less tangible philosophies north–south along the intermontane valleys of the Andes on the one hand, and east–west between the humid Amazon rainforest and the sun-baked Pacific coast on the other.

In the seventeenth century the Spanish chronicler Antonio Vasquez de Espinosa said of Chavín that it was a famous religious centre comparable to Rome or Jerusalem—in other words, it was still an important pilgrimage centre some hundred years after the Spanish conquest of the Inca empire and some two millennia after the demise of the Chavín culture itself. Pilgrimages to oracle sites were then, and still remain, an important feature of native Peruvian religious life. Today, of course, such 'journeys to god' have been heavily influenced by Roman Catholicism, brought to the Americas with zealous enthusiasm by the Spanish conquistadores. Many pilgrimages, however, still retain strong elements of Pre-Columbian belief.

At an altitude of 3,100 metres above sea-level, Chavín de Huántar is located in the Pukcha drainage system which is composed of the Mosna and Huari rivers, both of which drain eastwards into the Rio Marañon which subse-quently feeds into the great river system of the Amazon. To the west, it is bordered by the glaciated slopes of the aptly named Cordillera Blanca, and to the east lies the Cordillera Oriental.

At this altitude, and with an average rainfall of between 750 and 1,042 millimetres, the area is well suited to farming without the need for extensive irrigation. The reliable harvests produce maize, potatoes and a variety of other foodstuffs. Today the 30,000 hectares of good agricultural land, and some 80,000 hectares of pastoral land, for llamas and alpacas, support about 22,000 people, but, significantly, could feed a good deal more. A key to the agricultural success of this area is the fact that several distinct environmental zones lie within close proximity—there is only a two to three hours' walk between the irrigated valley floor, the potato fields on the upper slopes and the animal grazing pastures of the high, puna grassland. Chavín de Huántar thus lies

The semi-circular sunken plaza at Chavín de Huántar. *Photo, Sue Stoneman*

within an area which is characterised by what archaeologists and anthropologists alike refer to as a 'vertical archipelago' of food and resource producing zones.

Several previous investigators have called Chavín de Huántar an 'empty ceremonial centre', devoid of any great population, and housing just a small number of resident priests and craftsmen. This view, also applied at one time to both the Olmec and Classic Maya centres of Mexico, was the result of what, at the time, was thought to be the lack of any domestic living remains at the site. Indeed, Larco Hoyle commented that in his opinion Chavín was no more than a religious centre, a focus for pilgrimages and a mecca built to serve the feline cult.

In fact, as recent work has shown, Chavín de Huántar was both larger and more varied in its layout than many earlier reports had suggested. As was the case with the Olmec, archaeologists who once searched for and excavated within the monumental architecture, were only concerned with the large and impressive find. Only recently has archaeology concerned itself with 'social process' and attempted to discover how ancient centres worked and how the ordinary inhabitants lived. The evidence for Chavín having been far more than an empty ceremonial centre is now conclusive: both the Mosna and Huachecsa rivers had been canalised, and there are traces of a Chavín period stone bridge and extensive terracing adjacent to the ceremonial area. Whole sections of the site, some of which lie beneath the colonial period town, have revealed evidence of prehistoric housing and the practising of specialised crafts. Chavín de

Huántar certainly was an important religious centre, dominated by impressive architecture and adorned with startling imagery, but it also contained a sizeable and varied population.

Recent work by the archaeologist Richard Burger has clarified our picture of ancient Chavín de Huántar and has revealed its development as a site of both religious importance and population concentration. His detailed excavations suggest three distinct phases in its history.

The Urabarriu Phase, 850–460 BC

At this time Chavín de Huántar was a ceremonial centre with a small resident population. This phase saw the beginnings of Chavín civilisation, with people living on both sides of the Huachecsa river, linked by a bridge of cut and polished stone—which, incidentally, remained in use right up until 1945 when, sadly, it was swept away by one of the landslides which characterise this volcanically active region. The river itself was canalised with massive walls and drainage canals. Significantly, the bridge may well have been the secular focus of the site, as it both provided and controlled the strategically important access route east–west from the jungles of Amazonia to the Pacific coast.

During this early period the city was apparently divided into two distinct wards, a practice also found at the much later imperial Inca capital of Cuzco, where the physical division of living space had mythological as well as social implications. The upper section consisted of the sacred temple area with an adjacent section on the other side of the Huachecsa river; the lower section comprised living areas and a section of a massive wall. The two sections were separated by about half a kilometre of unoccupied land. This physical division—perhaps a sacred 'no-man's land'—may well have had ideological, mythological and social importance, reflecting cosmological concepts which divided different classes of Chavín society.

The lower section was concentrated around its northern wall, which was built of large boulders and ran east–west for about 110 metres, eventually connecting with an elevated causeway. This marked the limit of human occupation. Burger's view is that this great wall probably acted not only defensively but also to control access to Chavín from the lower Mosna river area and the lowlands and jungles beyond. Excavations here have revealed gallery-like buildings which may have been used for the storage of tribute, or perhaps tolls levied for access to the site. That the whole area was used as living space is indicated by the archaeological remains, which include bone tools, needles, awls and a variety of coarse stone-tools and domestic pottery.

The upper section was focused on the temple area with its imposing religious architecture. Whilst there is currently no link between the pottery found here and the superb range of stone-sculpted motifs which adorn the temple, Burger believes that the 'Old Temple' is the oldest major building at the site. There is also the less than conclusive, but nevertheless intriguing evidence which links Chavín's Urabarriu pottery with intricately carved bones from the site of

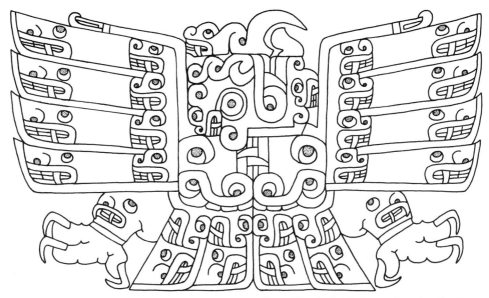

Composite jaguar-eagle relief from the New Temple at Chavín de Huántar. *Drawing, Pauline Stringfellow, after Rowe 1967, Fig. 11, p. 100*

Shillacoto, which display motifs similar to those carved as 'decoration' on the 'Old Temple'.

Despite the physical and perhaps 'cosmological' barrier between the upper and lower sections of the site, represented by the enigmatic strip of unoccupied land, exotic ceramics and marine shells are found scattered all over both areas, indicating a close integration of the various wards of the city and far-flung connections with other parts of Peru.

This earliest phase of Chavín's life has yielded the largest quantity of bone tools, and two of the recovered fragments have been identified as belonging to either the jaguar or puma. Burger's opinion is that jaguars do not occur at such high altitudes and that puma are rarely seen; he offers the opinion that these bones were especially acquired for bone-working, due to the symbolic importance and religious significance of large felines in the ideology of Chavín de Huántar. Within the temple area the inhabitants were apparently concerned primarily with the construction and maintenance of the religious buildings and the sacred rituals which took place there. In all probability, these elaborate religious ceremonies, the splendid paraphernalia of the priests and the impressive architecture gave Chavín a supernatural aura and added to its burgeoning prestige.

The Chakinani Phase, 460–390 BC

This succeeding period witnessed a major change in the settlement history of Chavín. The northernmost living quarters were abandoned and people clus-

Corner of the main Temple at Chavín de Huántar. *Photo, Sue Stoneman*

tered around the temple area on both banks of the Huachecsa river. This period was remarkably short-lived: fewer pottery fragments have been recovered, and the evidence for major building programmes in the ceremonial area is slight.

Due to the concentration of what had previously been two sections of Chavín, the overall population density increased in the temple quarter and the site extended to cover about 15 hectares. Chakinani pottery shows an increase in religiously inspired decoration, but exotic pottery types and food remains continue to suggest a high level of contact between the city and other more distant regions of Peru. At this time Chavín was possibly seeing the fruits of its growing reputation as a centre for pilgrimage, and was perhaps sucking in tribute and luxury goods from new areas. Certainly the first appearance of obsidian, that 'steel' of prehistory, occurs at Chavín during Chakinani times.

The Janabarriu Phase, 390–200 BC

During this final period of Chavín de Huántar's life the site expanded beyond the ideal size for a small ceremonial centre. The city now grew at a phenomenal rate to cover a maximum area of some 42 hectares. Living space was at a premium, occupation became ever denser, and even the mountain slopes to the west of the temple complex were occupied.

The Janabarriu period was a time of great activity and prosperity at Chavín, showing much renovation in terms of superimposed living floors, running repairs and additions to earlier buildings. The city was now four times the size it had been during its earliest period and had become one of the largest centres in the whole of Pre-Columbian America.

It must be said, however, that size alone is not all-important. There were other, larger sites in Peru earlier than Chavín, for example, Caballo Muerto on the adjacent Pacific coast. What makes Chavín de Huántar so important is not just its impressive overall size, but the internal organisation of the site and the craft specialisation of its inhabitants. For archaeologists these are crucial indicators that Chavín society was socially and economically well organised and divided.

When archaeologists look at the internal organisation of a prehistoric site they can discover who was doing what, where they were doing it and, with luck, why. At Chavín, for example, sector A yielded twice as much obsidian debris as sector D: this could be evidence for sector A having an artisan population who scraped and cleaned the skins of llama, alpaca and the various hunted animals. The residential flavour of this area was reinforced by the discovery of the foundations of rough houses with plain cooking and storage pottery wares. This evidence, combined with personal adornments of ear-spools, mirrors and bone needles, indicates that skilled craftsmen were organised along 'cottage indus-try' lines rather than in specialised workshops. The site was in fact an early example of a pre-industrial city. Such valuable insights into how ancient people lived and worked cannot be gauged from mere size alone.

In sector D, which was nearer to the sacred heart of the site, remains recovered from domestic refuse contained gold jewellery, esoteric materials such as fossils and the remains of salted fish. The area apparently housed a section of society which had a higher social status than sector A. This sector also yielded two caches of white and pink spondylus shells which had been worked by a skilled artisan. Whilst other, unworked shells came from the adjacent Peruvian coast—some 150 kilometres to the west, the ritually important spondylus shells were probably imported or traded in from coastal Ecuador, some 800 kilometres to the north. These shells were worked to produce a finished product of spondylus beads or pendants and were perhaps also sewn into the clothing of priest-rulers or used to decorate large wall-hangings for the temple itself. Shells decorated with typically Chavín motifs are well known.

During Janabarriu times Chavín society was both larger and, necessarily, better organised than in previous periods. The new buildings attached to the Old Temple, valley floor terracing and drainage were all public works requiring large amounts of well organised labour which, in all probability, came from the numerous small hamlets in the immediate hinterland of the site.

Janabarriu ceramics reveal a considerable amount of iconography, and this period sees the single largest quantity of typically Chavín style stone sculptures as well as the construction of the New Temple building. Also, a number of fragments of jet mirrors were discovered, and these were presumably of ritual importance, in much the same way that the polished haematite mirrors were to the Olmec rulers of Mexico's Gulf Coast.

The Testimony of Pottery

Until recently Chavín has attracted attention simply as a site with superb architectural features, and the pottery has been poorly served in terms of detailed investigation. As with Michael Coe's work at the Olmec centre of San Lorenzo, however, Richard Burger's expedition to Chavín had as a major objective the building up of a detailed analysis of the ceramics, in an attempt to tie them down to specific periods. Excavations by Julio Tello, and by the North American archaeologist Wendell Bennett during the 1940s, were not designed to produce an overall pottery sequence, and until the work of the Peruvian archaeologists Luis Lumbreras and Hernán Amat Olazabal in the late 'sixties and early 'seventies, Chavín's pottery was well documented but poorly understood.

These two archaeologists concentrated on the temple area, however, and so did not produce information which was applicable to the whole site. Their major breakthrough was to attempt to subdivide Chavín's pottery into a sequence of dated units. In practice, it proved far easier to identify two different groups of pottery rather than arrange them chronologically.

These two pottery types were called 'Ofrendas' and 'Rocas', the former being found in the maze of galleries within the temple structure and the latter in a disused drainage canal. Ofrendas pottery, dominated by curvilinear decoration in which felines or feline elements predominate, is only found within the galleries in which other ritual offerings were also discovered. Rocas ceramics, found mixed with fragments of bone, obsidian and stone, suggested to Lumbreras a strong contrast with the ritual context and decoration of Ofrendas. Few Rocas ceramics display feline decoration.

Burger's work has refined and clarified this picture. On the basis of decoration, Ofrendas pottery is now assigned to both the Urabarriu and Chakinani phases—that is, from 850–390 BC—and the Rocas pottery belongs to his Janabarriu phase—from 390–200 BC. Most of the pottery found by investigators previous to Burger is now assigned to this Janabarriu phase, lending weight to the idea that this period saw the greatest activity at the site.

The View over Chavín

The weight of evidence now strongly suggests that in the earliest, Urabarriu phase, Chavín was indeed a small ceremonial centre possessing a resident population of perhaps 200 people; this increased in the succeeding Chakinani period, but the city only developed into a major religious and population centre during Janabarriu times.

Based on the 1972 census and making allowances for areas known to be less densely populated, Burger has estimated that the population of ancient Chavín de Huántar could have been in the region of 2,000–3,000 people at its height. Even at its peak, however, the resident population was never large enough to have undertaken its large building programmes. Chavín de Huántar depended on the surrounding hamlets and villages for both manpower and food. This vertical grading of environmental zones included areas of tuber-growing on the slopes and llama and alpaca herding up on the high grassland pastures. The villages of each area contributed food and material resources characteristic of their respective locations.

Three examples of such support villages are known archaeologically— Pojoc, Waman Wain and Aljapuquio—and all have deeply buried levels containing typical Chavín pottery of the Urabarriu phase. Many other such hamlets must have existed, and some are known from the valley floor area around Chavín itself. Whilst individually small, collectively such villages probably accounted for the majority of the population in Chavín times. Even in 1961, such scattered villages housed some 87 per cent of the local population of the area, and the same was probably true in Chavín's heyday.

Just as, in the case of the Olmec, La Venta and San Lorenzo were ceremonial centres supported by the manpower, food and tribute of the surrounding agricultural villages, so Chavín benefited from the efforts of its dispersed populations. These villages would have supplied seasonal food and labour and, under the direction of the elite, would have constructed the monumental buildings so important to the sacred nature of the site. Right up until the first half of the twentieth century, the surrounding villages sent labourers to the Colonial period town of Chavín de Huántar to help in the building

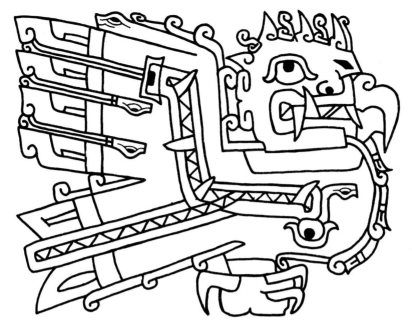

Profile of a felinised harpy eagle from the Black and White Portal at Chavín. *Drawing, Pauline Stringfellow, after Rowe 1967, Fig. 16, p. 102*

and maintenance of the village church and town hall—public works which paralleled the sacred and secular buildings of the ancient site. Such explanations are more likely than Larco Hoyle's suggestion of pilgrims making their arduous way up from the coast for several weeks in order to build the great monuments at Chavín. Today, as in the past, the local support area of Chavín lies more or less within two days' walking distance of the site.

The Peruvian Perspective

Over recent years archaeologists have realised that Tello's concept of Chavín as the inspiration for, and dominant example of, Peruvian civilisation was woefully inadequate. Sophisticated ancient cultures, often occupying large prehistoric centres, had existed during the earlier Preceramic and Initial periods, especially between *c.* 2000 and 1000 BC.

This reassessment derives partly from the progress of archaeological investigation. Today many more sites belonging particularly to the Initial Period of the second millennium BC have been studied and a wider, more detailed and balanced perspective has resulted. For example, at the site of La Florida in the Rimac valley, the construction of a huge U-shaped platform was under way before 2150 BC. The building of La Florida required almost seven million man-days, and the necessary labour force would have had to be drawn not just from the Rimac valley itself, but from the adjacent Chillón and Lurín valleys as well.

The main pyramid at Sechín Alto, in the Casma valley, was built mostly during the Initial Period, and is some 15 times larger than the main temple at Chavín de Huántar. The whole site extends over some 400 hectares. Also in the Casma valley is the famous site of Cerro Sechín, home of that gruesome repertoire of stone carvings, and now dated to about 1300 BC. Just 20 kilometres south of the Casma valley lies the huge and impressive Initial Period site of Las Haldas, whose main building is a multistepped, terraced platform, dated to between 1600 and 1400 BC and surrounded by no less than seventeen smaller pyramids. In addition to the main construction are four aligned rectangular plazas, and several sunken circular courts.

These huge coastal centres, along with other important highland sites such as La Galgada, Huaricoto and Shillacoto, have forced a reappraisal of the origins and development of Peruvian civilisation. A new framework is being built on this recent evidence and the restrictive shackles of Tello's earlier concept have been broken. Even some of the older discoveries from such Andean sites as Kotosh and Pacopampa are now revealing pre-Chavín dates and thus their true significance. Such advances, when combined with Burger's re-dating of Chavín's beginnings, from c. 1200 to c. 850 BC, have led to a challenging time in the archaeology of early Peruvian civilisation.

Impressive as its forebears were, however, Chavín de Huántar was undoubtedly the major cultural force during the Early Horizon, from 900 to 200 BC. Substantially larger than any other contemporary centre known from the central highlands, it may well have been one of the largest centres in all Peru at this time. Its size, internal organisation, skilled craftsmen and the elite priest-rulers who controlled it, reworked the achievements of previous cultures to forge a unique ideology which spread the length and breadth of early Peru. The striking images of its art style struck a responsive chord and became the graphic expression of a potent religious movement which exercised a lasting effect on ancient Peruvian society in a way which its predecessors had failed to do.

The great effect wrought by Chavín on its prehistoric contemporaries is clearly visible in the archaeological record. Political, economic and perhaps ideological relations between the major regional centres underwent dramatic upheaval, and previous architectural styles now changed under its pervasive influence. Local pottery traditions were disrupted and the distinctive and religiously inspired iconography of Chavín began to invade previously local assemblages. During the fifth century BC this whole process was reinforced by the dramatic decline of many of the great coastal centres.

We have to ask, however, as we did with the Olmec: what were these artistic motifs, these symbols of power which so graphically expressed Chavín's ideology and which so impressed the rest of Peru's prehistoric peoples? The answer lies in the content and style of the art which decorated the monumental buildings and small artefacts alike, and which in turn enable us to link the practical with the esoteric, to suggest a connection between economic activity, religion, ideology and the nature of society. Once again the recurring imagery of the feline plays a dramatic and central role.

CHAPTER 6

CHAVÍN ART, RELIGION AND SOCIETY

Startling images carved in stone, cast in gold or worked in textiles or pottery have hitherto been the main claim to fame of the Chavín civilisation. Such images do not stand alone as splendid but isolated pieces of Pre-Columbian art: across the millennia they speak to us of the technological and aesthetic sophistication of their indigenous creators, providing dramatic insights into the type of society which produced them.

The art of Chavín is inextricably bound to the nature of Chavín society, its origins, religion, ideology and technological expertise. It provides lasting evidence of the great cultural achievements of ancient Peruvian civilisation which flourished in an oral tradition only, without benefit of writing, for more than three and a half thousand years. It creates dramatic images of the past, sometimes immediately recognisable, often strangely exotic, but always full of undeciphered information. Decoding the mythic and metaphorical message of Chavín art is one of the main tasks of the archaeologist, aided increasingly by a range of other specialists including anthropologists, botanists and zoologists.

Although the artists of Chavín lived in our world, they nevertheless inhabited an 'alternative' universe whose people, animals and natural surroundings were infused with supernatural power and believed to possess human-like 'souls' and motivations. Chavín art, in common with all Pre-Columbian artistic endeavour, must be viewed from an Amerindian rather than a Western perspective: only in this way can we begin to unravel the complex thread of culture that binds us to the past.

Art, Culture and the Amazonian Connection

The place of Chavín de Huántar in the overall context of Peruvian prehistory has already been discussed. But what of the art, both monumental and small-scale, for which the site has been justly famous for so long? At none of the earlier large coastal sites do we find such a sophisticated style, executed in such a wide variety of media and forcefully expressing the ideology of a local cult centre.

Whilst Chavín de Huántar lies, as we have seen, in the stark beauty of the Andes, its art style has a strong Amazonian flavour. The animals so expertly portrayed are not the Andean condor, puma or llama, but the harpy eagle, jaguar and cayman. Indeed, as Donald Lathrap, a North American archaeologist who has written extensively on the subject, has pointed out, almost all of the animals depicted in the distinctive Chavín style come not from the high sierra, but are native to the steaming jungles of the Amazon rainforest. This is both significant and intriguing, for whilst Chavín civilisation was an Andean phenomenon, the creatures which adorn its sophisticated art and architecture are those most commonly found in a region populated by smaller, tribal societies. Chavín's temples may have housed a priesthood, but from the artistic evidence they must have looked for all the world like the shamans and sorcerers of forest tribes.

Chavín appears as a theocratic civilisation, deriving its importance, prestige and 'sacred power' from its priests' access to the supernatural realm of ancestors, animal spirits and supernatural forces. This special relationship between priest and spirit is indicated repeatedly by the many dramatic portrayals of forest animals and strange beings, half-human, half-animal, which straddle the boundaries between the physical and metaphysical worlds. At Chavín, for the first time in the Andes, we have powerful depictions of shamans in their supernatural disguises, carved in stone, painted on textiles and thus made both imposing and permanent.

Edge of the Jungle

At the site of Kotosh on the eastern slopes of the Andes, in an area known as the Ceja de Montaña, or Cloud Forest, there is an early cult centre situated on the right bank of the Higueras river. Kotosh is a precociously early highland site, composed of two artificial mounds and three stone-built constructions spanning, throughout its complex development, both pre-ceramic and ceramic phases. The edge of the tropical forest lies only some 35 kilometres away.

The earliest occupation at the site is the pre-ceramic 'Mito' phase, during which several courts and the 'Temple of the Crossed Hands' were built. The latter is so-called because of its famous plaster relief, found on the inner wall of the building. Next came the 'Wairajirca' phase, dated at around 1850 BC. Whilst architecturally there appears to have been no sudden break with previous traditions, this period yielded the first evidence of pottery at the site. In the succeeding 'Kotosh' phase (with radiocarbon dates of 1120 and 890 BC), there are indications that maize was introduced. Following this, Kotosh's 'Chavín' phase left archaeological remains characterised by almost purely Chavín designs in pottery, gold and bone. At this time newer, larger buildings were constructed and smothered with red paint.

Some investigators believe that a feline cult began during the Wairajirca phase, and pottery from this time depicts felines, snakes and owls in a realistic rather than anthropomorphic fashion. It was Julio Tello who, in 1935, first suggested that the decoration on Wairajirca phase pottery may have derived from the eastern jungles. In the succeeding Kotosh period, representations of 'cat-men' appear, indicating a change to anthropomorphism in religious

The plaster relief of the Crossed Hands from the earliest levels of occupation at Kotosh in the eastern Andes. *Photo, Author*

beliefs. As Kotosh is nearer to the Amazon than Chavín, it may have received stronger religious influences relating to shamans and the forest predators, so important in the spiritual life of jungle inhabitants. Nevertheless, whilst Kotosh may have been an important staging-post in the arrival of tropical rainforest beliefs at Chavín, the art style developed within the Andes, at Chavín itself.

East of Kotosh, where the foothills of the Andes fall away into the wide Amazon basin, the region is dominated geographically by the Ucayali river, which flows northwards to join the Marañon river and thus forms the great Amazon fluvial system. During the late 1950s, Donald Lathrap excavated at a site named Tutishcainyo, situated near an oxbow lake at Yarinacocha, north-west of the modern Peruvian jungle town of Pucallpa. Here he discovered the remains of an ancient riverside village with pottery ornamented with U-shaped incisions and rectilinear designs. The only non-geometric decoration was that of a cat-head incised on an oval bowl. This represents perhaps the earliest depiction of the feline motif in Peruvian art.

Significantly, there are technological and stylistic similarities over a long period in the pottery found at the two sites—between the early Tutishcainyo wares and the earliest pottery phase at Kotosh, Wairajirca, and also between the late Tutishcainyo deposits and the 'Kotosh' phase at Kotosh. These links were further strengthened with the discovery of what Lathrap called Shakimu pottery in an area near to the Tutishcainyo site.

Shakimu pottery, dated to *c.* 650 BC, is thought to be a development from the previous Tutishcainyo tradition but also includes a number of vessels carved with intricate designs and covered with red paint before firing. According to Lathrap, these exotic ceramics are strongly influenced by the Chavín style emanating from the Andes to the west. The Shakimu people seem to have been imitating the Chavín style at least in one particular type of their pottery, suggesting a long prehistory of contact between the Amazon and the Andes, during which ideas, art styles, techniques and ideologies travelled freely between the two regions.

Jungle Denizens at Chavín

Evidence for the jungle origin of the animals so frequently depicted at Chavín de Huántar is pervasive. Even though many are fantastically created and portray mythological creatures, some important facts emerge. It was the real animals of the jungle, with their natural appearance, behaviour and actual or metaphorical qualities, which provided the native inhabitants with the raw material for their ideas, beliefs and artistic designs. Human societies observe, select and manipulate those aspects of their natural environment which appear useful and meaningful in expressing social relations between people.

The Jaguar is the largest cat in the New World. Its predatory nature, strength and agility make it an ideal choice for portraying such human qualities as success in hunting, warfare and, on a more subtle level, supernatural protection against spirit attack—whether from malevolent forest spirits, from illness or from the shamans of other tribes. Time and again the images at Chavín repeat the feline form, sometimes naturalistically but more often combined with human and bird characteristics—mixing, as it were, the vital features of each. Whilst it is clearly impossible to insist that all feline images at Chavín are jaguar and not puma, those showing a naturalistically rendered feline often bear the characteristic rosettes which make the jaguar's appearance so distinctively different from the plain silvery-brown coat of the puma.

The jaguar is the tropical forest's dominant predator. It occupies the top of the food chain, hunting and killing all manner of lesser animals. Its obvious success in hunting has led many forest tribes to call it the supreme hunter and the 'one' who controls the very life-force of the jungle. From being the most important creature in the natural world it is transformed in the Amerindian mind to the dominant force in the shape-changing world of the supernatural. As it is the concept of humans 'becoming jaguars' which is important, we can begin to understand why Chavín's artisans concentrated their efforts on portraying half-human, half-feline creatures rather than simply depicting felines in their natural form.

The bird representations at Chavín are, most likely, not condors but harpy eagles (*Harpia harpyja*). This fierce raptorial bird is a monkey eater and is restricted in range to areas which support its prey—the tropical forests. Harpy eagles are the most impressive and powerful predatory birds in South America and in the cosmologies of lowland tribes occupy an important position in religious belief and ritual. In many ways the harpy eagle can be seen as the supreme airborne predator, the 'jaguar' of the skies, and indeed, several Indian groups refer to this impressive bird of prey in exactly these terms. To create a composite jaguar-eagle creature, as the artisans at Chavín did so convincingly, becomes understandable in a world-view where concepts of hunting, ferocity and strength were intertwined.

Art and Architecture

The artistic elements which make up the unique Chavín art style have been selected, re-combined and executed in an equally distinctive manner and with what the renowned Andeanist John Rowe has called the conventions of 'symmetry' and 'repetition'. Typically Chavín features are the eccentric eyes peering, as it were, upwards to the celestial sphere. Two types of eye motif are found: a circular one which appears only on the more realistically depicted felines, and a rectangular variant which appears in later sculptures and, less frequently, on naturalistic portrayals. Eyes are full of metaphorical significance for native Amerindians: they enable shamans to perceive the otherwise invisible spirits, they are linked closely to mirrors and ideas of reflection and they emit tears, which are often seen as analogous to rain and so linked to the concept of fertility.

It is surely significant that the commonest device found in Chavín art is the replacement of the human and animal mouth with that of a jaguar's snarling muzzle and bared fangs. The idea that the snarling cat mouth was a power symbol in its own right may be seen in the 'need' to felinise non-cat figures. All sculpture possessing the cat-mouth is temple sculpture, and we may therefore be witnessing an iconography of power in which individual aspects of the jaguar, as the most mythologically important animal, are torn from their natural context and recombined in a composite figure in a way which made perfect sense both to the inhabitants of Chavín de Huántar and the pilgrims who journeyed there. As Rowe says, perhaps the very presence of the cat-mouth on a sculpture indicates that the creature is a supernatural being.

In Chavín art, feline mouths are depicted both frontally and in profile, and are found on many of the site's most impressive sculptures. Both the Lanzón and the unique group of tenoned heads have large mouths with upturned corners and emerging upper fangs. Another variation is the so-called U-shaped mouth, with curving fangs on either side, which some authorities believe can be traced to the pre-Chavín Wairajirca style at Kotosh. This U-shaped mouth becomes more common later in the Chavín period and is found on the elaborate carving of the Raimondi stela, as well as on textiles from Peru's arid south coast. Like the eyes, the mouth is not only highly distinctive in execution but also significant in terms of Amerindian thought. Jaguar mouths and fangs are

Carved stone head showing feline fangs and large staring eyes, from Chavín de Huántar.
Photo, Tony Morrison, South American Pictures

power-symbols amongst Amazonian societies where shamans and sorcerers often wear bracelets and necklaces of jaguar fangs in the belief that they will thus acquire the ferocity of the beast.

The highly decorated coat of the jaguar also provided the artisans of Chavín with raw material for artistic elaboration, and various interpretations of the animal's dark-brown rosettes found their way into the artistic repertoire. Circle-and-dot, L-shape, spiral, cloud-shape, S-shape, cross and figure '8' are all found on the body of feline stone-carvings, as well as on a variety of Chavín pottery.

Another artistic convention was the substitution of serpents for body hair, especially around the eyes. John Rowe has labelled such substitutions 'kennings', after a literary device common in Old Norse court poetry. The idea that hair was 'kenned' as serpents is linked to the concept of metaphor— implying that everyone understood the allusions. Rowe gives the example that, whilst we may say of a woman that she has 'snaky hair', we can go further and refer to her hair as 'her nest of snakes'—a substitution which does not mention hair at all and is a prime example of the use of kennings. For the Chavín artists, the substitution of snakes for hair may have possessed a deepfelt significance which today we can only guess at. From the anthropological point of view, body hair and serpents possess strong sexual overtones, linked once again to fertility.

In addition, tropical rainforest societies often think of serpents as the supernatural animal familiars or spirit-helpers of the jaguar and of the shaman who 'turns into' a jaguar.

The feline is obviously important in Chavín art because depictions of the animal, either whole or in part, are present throughout its range. Most are shown in profile, the single most dramatic example being the spectacular group of jaguars and supernatural beings, carved in bas-relief, which forms the architectural boundary to the circular sunken court discovered in 1972 by the Peruvian archaeologist Luís Lumbreras. Clearly associated with the Old Temple, this impressive plaza had a perimeter formed by two parallel levels of low-relief carvings. On the north side, the lower panel was originally made up of perhaps fourteen beautifully rendered jaguars carved in profile. On the upper panel were possibly the same number of anthropomorphic figures, most of which were heavily worn away. The latter possess a typical snarling mouth, bared fangs, clawed hands and serpents substituted for hair. This spectacular discovery portrayed in no uncertain terms the fascination of Chavín artists with the jaguar: in one piece of architecture we have both naturally rendered felines and supernatural jaguar-like beings.

Depictions of Chavín felines in the round are comparatively rare, the beautifully carved cat-mortar, currently held at Pennsylvania Museum, being the most famous example. Similar feline-shaped mortars have been found elsewhere, especially at another great highland site, Pacopampa.

Ubiquitous in stone sculpture, the image of the jaguar is also found on the extraordinary range of Chavín ceramics which were excavated from the early 1930s until the late 1970s. During 1934 Julio Tello, the discoverer of Chavín, retrieved pottery whose artistic decoration he compared with the site's impressive stone sculpture, offering the explanation that all Chavín art portrayed mythological demons. During the 1940s the North American archaeologist Wendell Bennett excavated a series of pits which yielded almost

The Pennsylvania mortar, a jaguar effigy in Chavín style, possibly used for grinding narcotic snuff. *Photo, The University Museum, University of Pennsylvania.*

3,000 pieces of pottery, including two complete vessels. However, it was the work of Luís Lumbreras and his collaborators which first began to identify different decorative styles and motifs in Chavín pottery.

On the basis of investigations carried out during the 1960s and '70s Lumbreras identified two distinct types which he called 'Ofrendas' and 'Rocas'. Ofrendas ceramics (*ofrendas* being Spanish for 'offerings') were found in the sacred location of the maze of galleries in the temple building which housed the 'Smiling God' of the Lanzón. This pottery was beautifully made, with curvilinear decoration in which felines, or feline elements in the service of mythological creatures, predominated. Ceramic bowls and bottles with elongated spouts portray a mythological person who can be compared to the Tello obelisk. Feline fangs and mouths appear in a swirl of twining images—a kind of symbolic shorthand forced on the potter by the material itself. Polished grey bowls in particular are famous for their depictions of spotted jaguars and composite jaguar-eagles.

The location of the Ofrendas pottery was also significant. Within the temple they are reported to have been found intact along the interior walls of the galleries, together with such exotic food offerings as shells and fish bones, suggesting that they may have been especially made for ritual use inside the holy temple. Indeed, at the centre of these offerings was a woman's skull, surrounded by a ring of a child's teeth.

Rocas ceramics, in contrast, were found in a disused drainage canal. The wares are solid and stone-like in appearance, hence their name, and few display feline decoration. Where they do occur, however, feline designs are by and large less sophisticated in their execution than those of Ofrendas.

Chavín de Huántar is often regarded as the artistic archetype of the Early Horizon in Peru, influencing many other contemporary and subsequent cultures. The most important focus of the ceremonial part of the site is the Old Temple. Consisting of a group of rectangular buildings, some up to 12 metres high, it is honeycombed with interior passages or galleries linking a series of small rooms and possessing an elaborate system of ventilation shafts. The outside walls were originally decorated with intricately carved stone heads depicting anthropomorphic creatures—half human and half feline, often with curling serpents replacing hair and eyebrows. Tenoned into the wall and possibly painted, some of these intriguing stone heads have since disappeared. Today others lie within the temple galleries, whilst further examples were recently discovered during the same excavations which uncovered the sunken circular plaza. Above this strange row of fantastical stone heads was a projecting cornice of flat slabs carved with low-relief figures—these have now fallen away to be found at the foot of the building.

One of the maze of interior galleries leads evocatively to a great stone sculpture. This awe-inspiring monolithic image is carved from a shaft of white granite some 4.53 metres tall, and is commonly referred to as the 'Lanzón' because of its lance-like shape. In all probability it was the earliest principal cult object and stands close to the central axis of the oldest part of the temple.

The only remaining felinised carved stone head in its original position, tenoned into the outside of the Lanzón Temple at Chavín de Huántar. *Photo, Sue Stoneman*

Still occupying its original setting, its size and position suggest that the whole temple structure may have been built around it. The anthropomorphic deity represented on the Lanzón may have been enshrined in its own temple-mausoleum as a deified shaman-priest or mythological ancestor of the Chavín people.

The Lanzón is basically human in form, possessing artistic elaborations of typically Chavín style. The left arm rests by its side, while the right is raised and the fingers end in long nails which appear as sharp, cat-like claws. The face itself reveals heavy feline influence, with a wide, upturned mouth from which two massive fangs emerge. Hair is once again represented by serpents and the figure wears a girdle of small feline heads.

Originally U-shaped, with a main building and two projecting wings, the Old Temple enclosed a rectangular court on three sides, leaving open the direction of sunrise and the tropical forest to the east. This first building was subsequently enlarged, mainly towards the south wing which then became the new focus of religious activity. Along with this extension a new and larger court was laid out in front, with flanking buildings to the north and south again creating the apparently significant U-shaped arrangement open to the east. The eastern front of this new building was provided with an impressive monumental doorway, the southern part of white granite and the northern half of black limestone, which has been pragmatically labelled by archaeologists the 'Black and White Portal'.

The artistic decoration of the doorway is both impressive and significant, the two cylindrical stone columns being covered with depictions of birds of prey. John Rowe, in his detailed study of the form and meaning of Chavín art,

Lateral view of 'El Lanzón'. Carved of white granite and some four and a half metres tall, it depicts an anthropomorphic being with upward-gazing eyes, prominent fangs, serpent hair and elaborate headdress consisting of feline snarling faces in profile. *Drawing, Pauline Stringfellow, after Rowe 1967, Fig. 5*

described these low-relief carvings as having the body, legs and arms of a human, and the head, wings and claws of raptorial birds—an eagle on the south column and a hawk on the north. He interpreted these designs as messengers or guardians of the supernatural gods worshipped inside the main temple. Others have suggested that the images portray the twin male/female essences in a time-honoured Andean tradition of dual representation.

Another justly famous Chavín sculpture is that known as the Raimondi stone. Found in the temple ruins in 1840, it is a beautifully rendered granite slab carved in low relief, and at 198 centimetres long by 74 centimetres wide, is the largest relief slab showing a single figure ever found at the site. The Raimondi stone shows a standing human form clasping two staffs, and for this reason is often referred to as the 'Staff God'. These staffs themselves are heavily decorated with feline heads and cat-mouths with crossed fangs. The mouth of the Staff God is turned downwards, and both upper and lower canines protrude from its snarling lips. Of its whole length, the body of this supernatural being occupies only the lower third, the remaining two thirds being taken up with the elaborate headdress or coiffure composed of twining serpents. For John Rowe this Staff God represents the major deity of the more recently constructed New Temple, whose images are found beyond Chavín de Huántar itself—most notably on small pieces of goldwork from Chongoyape on Peru's north coast, and on a number of painted textiles from the south coast.

Perhaps the piece of Chavín stone sculpture which has received most scholarly attention, however, is the rectangular shaft of carved granite called the 'Tello Obelisk', in honour of the famous Peruvianist. Carved on all four sides, its central design consists of two representations of a mythical being, designated Cayman A and Cayman B.

Tello himself referred to the obelisk as a 'cat' or 'cat-dragon', but John Rowe regarded it as a cayman, a species of New World crocodile. Donald Lathrap, who has taken a special interest in this sculpture, agrees with Rowe, identifying the creature as the black cayman (*Melanosuchus niger*), because the full set of upper teeth are visible despite the mouth being firmly shut— a characteristic feature of crocodilians. To the casual observer, however, these two figures could easily represent a feline monster.

Somewhat, strangely, the obelisk has the tail of a fish and is surrounded by other reminders of a watery environment—for example, a mollusc above the snout of Cayman A. Lathrap has interpreted this figure as the great cayman of the watery underworld. Towards the top of Cayman B is a raptorial bird, most probably the harpy eagle, and this he has identified as the great cayman of the sky.

However, a close examination of this intriguing and complex masterpiece suggests that Tello may have been at least half right after all, for images of the jaguar abound on the obelisk. The mollusc above Cayman A has a feline mouth, and the raptorial bird above Cayman B may be the 'jaguar of the skies', since we know from modern Amazonian societies that the beak and talons of the harpy eagle are regarded as analogous to the fangs and claws of the jaguar. In addition, there is a beautifully carved jaguar on Cayman A which significantly overlaps onto the main cayman figure, and a number of miscellaneous feline heads and mouths scattered all over the sculpture. Several plants, variously identified as bottlegourds, aji peppers and maize, emerge from feline mouths, and Cayman A has a cat head peeping from its clawed hind foot. Perhaps most significant, however, is the fact that, contrary to what some authorities have argued, the cayman is not regarded as the most powerful and important creature of watery environments, nor does it alone signify concepts of water and fertility.

The accounts of everyday life and religious belief amongst Amazonian Indian tribes indicate, often in great detail, that the jaguar is the 'Master of Animals', and controls the rain, the watery depths and fertility. Its roar presages rain and the consequent swelling of rivers and lakes. Travellers' accounts, old and new, tell of jaguars attacking and eating caymans, and several illustrations of such dramatic confrontations exist. Whilst we can accept the cayman as dangerous, powerful and important in indigenous beliefs, we must also recognise that its predator in the real world is the jaguar. Moving from the real to the supernatural and mythic world, the jaguar is therefore 'Master' of the cayman. The frequency of feline characteristics, heads and mouths on the Tello Obelisk may allow for a re-interpretation of this monolithic sculpture as a jaguar-cayman, another product of the Amerindian mind, rather than simply a naturalistic portrayal of one particular animal.

Cult and Religion

Whilst it is always dangerous to use modern analogies to explain the enigmas of archaeology, such methods may be used in the New World, albeit with care, due to the long continuity of thought, belief, language and culture. Recent work by anthropologists, botanists and zoologists has thrown fresh light on the nature and workings of ancient societies whose art styles have preserved much that they considered important. This is certainly the case with Chavín and its rich corpus of artistic motifs.

The two major deities of Chavín, the so-called 'Smiling God' of the Lanzón and the 'Staff God' of the Raimondi stela, represent supernatural beings which are in essence anthropomorphised felines—a human torso with feline head, snarling mouth, fangs and clawed hands and feet. It is surely significant that one of the best preserved of the anthropomorphic figures from the upper register of the sunken circular plaza is shown grasping what appears to be a ribbed cactus. This has recently been identified as the powerful hallucinogenic San Pedro (*Trichocereus pachanoi*) which, despite the passage of two and a half millennia is still used today by the inheritors of the shamanic tradition—folk-curers called *curanderos*.

In his book *The Wizard of the Four Winds*, the anthropologist Douglas Sharon has written a detailed study of this cactus and its use in shamanic curing by Eduardo Calderón, a noted Peruvian *curandero*. The San Pedro cactus contains

Stone bas-relief of a jaguar-being or shaman/priest with jaguar and serpent regalia, grasping what may be the hallucinogenic San Pedro cactus. *Drawing, Pauline Stringfellow, after Roe 1978, Fig. 1*

the potent alkaloid mescaline and strongly alters the state of consciousness of those who partake of it, producing multicoloured visions in a kaleidoscope of shapes and patterns. Calderón, like the shamans of prehistoric times, uses the cactus to see into the spirit world and diagnose the causes of and cures for illness. As the most powerful of South American hallucinogens, the San Pedro is considered not only medicinal but 'magical' and is thought to talk to those who know how to use it. Under the influence of the San Pedro the *curandero* is able to do battle with ferocious animals, to travel back and forth in a sort of dreamtime and to comprehend the mysteries of life.

The presence of the San Pedro cactus on the stone reliefs at Chavín is a firm indication that beliefs in the magical and transformational power of certain plants is no recent invention or discovery. Whilst Eduardo Calderón is a folk-curer living in a twentieth century surrounded by modern and scientific medicine, the power of narcotic plants in prehistoric times must have seemed miraculous evidence of the power and prestige of the shamans and priests who knew how to use them. The linked images of the jaguar, the San Pedro and strange half-human, half-animal creatures which may represent a shaman or priest 'transformed' into a jaguar, give us an important insight into the strange world which the people of Chavín inhabited.

Evidence that Chavín religion was essentially shamanistic is also found in such artistic media as textiles and pottery. On a fragment of painted textile from Karwa, in the Ica valley on Peru's south coast, there are no less than five representations of the San Pedro cactus, one of which is directly associated with a spotted feline and the partial image of a Staff God. There are also beautifully modelled representations of spotted cats with cacti in Tembladera pottery, a coastal variation of the Chavín style. Such pottery shows not only spotted felines and cacti, but also heavily incised figures of supernatural creatures straight out of the Chavín pantheon in the adjacent highlands,

Shamans have been recorded as saying that certain varieties of hallucinogenic plants will transform them into fierce, predatory jaguars— strong, wily, resourceful and able to do battle with supernatural forces. Such beliefs are so widespread in South America that they may well have persisted since prehistoric times and been prevalent in Chavín society between 850 and 400 BC. We can envisage the famous Pennsylvania Museum cat-mortar being used ceremonially to grind various narcotic preparations for ritual consumption in the cabalistic ceremonies which took place within the precincts of the sacred temple. Here, surrounded by the dimly lit feline imagery of the intricate wall hangings, stone sculpture and pottery, narcotic drugs would have been taken to transform the priest into a supernatural jaguar. Their preparation in a jaguar-shaped mortar would have piled symbolism upon symbolism, uniting more closely the identity of the human priest with the soul or essence of the sacred animal.

A Precocious Technology?

Although it is dangerous to attempt to construct too full a picture of a society from the dead bones of its archaeological remains, significant facts do emerge from the wealth of data we now possess on Chavín. It is probably no co-incidence that the appearance of such a sophisticated art style, along with its ideological message, was paralleled by an astonishing increase in the range of technological achievements, all firmly stamped with the distinctive mark of Chavín art.

Amongst the new inventions were the creation of textile paints, the first extensive use of llama and alpaca hair in textiles, the first use of textiles as surfaces for painted designs, and the textile manufacturing techniques of looping and discontinuous weft.

It is the painted textiles that reveal most about these 'high-tech' advances during Chavín times. The spur to this advance, like many in prehistory, was not simply a search for new and ever more efficient ways of doing things, but rather new ways in which the ideological message encoded in the art style could be conveyed. A surviving fragment of a large circular textile illustrates paired facing jaguars conceptually and stylistically similar to the carved stone jaguar designs on the sunken plaza at Chavín.

After the Chavín period, similarly painted and decorated textiles are found in all periods of Peruvian prehistory. The sheer scale is often daunting—some are 2.72 metres high and three metres long, much too large to be worn as clothing and their painted surfaces far too delicate for outdoor use. The lack of archaeological evidence that they were ever used as mummy wrappings, combined with their horizontal warp, suggests that they may have been held

Fragment of a painted cotton wall-hanging, from the Ica Valley, southern Peru. Showing Chavín-style feline faces with fang and snake motifs. Height 90 cms, width 63 cms. *Photo, Courtesy of Dumbarton Oaks Research Library and Collections, Washington, D.C.*

upright with vertical poles, perhaps serving as temple wall-hangings. The artistic message they carried—naturalistically portrayed feline images and/or half-human, half-feline beings—would have made a dramatic backdrop to the highly charged atmosphere of Chavín rituals.

Some authorities believe that the purity of style in many of these textile fragments indicate that they were all made in one place, possibly at Chavín de Huántar itself, and subsequently taken to other parts of Peru where, due to the drier climate they have better survived the passage of centuries.

The cultural and psychological effect of seeing a well-known motif—that is, the jaguar or 'jaguarised humans'—appear in newly invented and visually impressive media can today only be guessed at. However, in our own time, the effect of superior technology on a nation's prestige and 'power' is well known. Images of religion are transferrable from one medium to another, and the more sophisticated the medium, the more omnipotent the message may appear.

Besides the advances in textile production and its religious and economic connotations—still evident more than 1,500 years later when the Inca state organised vast production and storage of textiles—technological advances also included metallurgy, especially goldworking. As we have seen, a rich collection of gold ornaments of Chavín style were found at Chongoyape on Peru's north coast. In fact there were two distinct discoveries at Chongoyape, but they are often lumped together as examples of Chavín influence or control of this coastal region.

The Chongoyape finds included three cylindrical gold crowns, a headband (significantly of the same circumference as the crowns, suggesting that all may have been worn by the same individual), tweezers and earspools. Both the crowns and earspools were decorated in *repoussé* Chavín style—one crown depicting a feline/human head in profile with typically crossed fangs, eccentric eyes and associated serpents; another bearing an anthropomorphic feline standing face-on and holding two staffs, with a stylised feline face on its chest. Other finds included pottery, a stone bowl and a jet mirror. The sophistication of this metalwork indicates a high level of technological achievement, but once again the techniques had been used to display Chavín ideology, centred on the connection between humans and felines. Whilst eminently civilised in technique, the effect remains shamanistic.

Jaguars in Chavín Art

Like all Pre-Columbian art, Chavín designs were not intended to be simply decorative. In the absence of writing, images conveyed information, carried a message and invoked an emotional response. Chavín art has been justly famous since the site's discovery, yet only now are we beginning to comprehend its significance—to the extent that is possible when studying the evidence of a prehistoric civilisation. As we look at the anthropological, zoological and botanical images and attempt to decode their message, we are drawn to the conclusion that they reveal a society which, despite the evident sophistication of its architecture, planning, organisation, arts and crafts, still clung to a world-view that was basically shamanistic and Amazonian.

The depiction of naturalistically rendered jaguars, birds, butterflies and serpents went alongside the creation of a pantheon of impossible and fantastic creatures, which were either composites of real animals or strangely anthropomorphic. To the people of Chavín they were as recognisable and understandable as they are incomprehensible to us.

Whilst the origins of Chavín's religious beliefs may lie in the Amazon, there can be no doubt that, as an Andean phenomenon, its society was firmly within the orbit of civilisation which embraced the earlier huge coastal centres. Chavín de Huántar appears to have drawn together many different strands of culture from the widely differing regions of ancient Peru, and in doing so it created something new—a sophisticated art style which expressed age-old beliefs in dramatically new ways. Chavín artists crystallised belief and technology, they transformed the visions of the shaman into stone, the most permanent medium at their disposal. By so doing they bequeathed to subsequent civilisations a cosmic vision of a universe where the boundary between life and death was permeable, and where animals and humans associated in a dazzling array of fantastic shape and form.

Whilst the ultimate key to understanding Chavín art lies buried beyond recovery in the minds of its creators, we can still dimly perceive its motivating forces amongst the scattered remnants of tropical forest Indian societies, which have managed to preserve their traditional way of life almost to the verge of the twenty-first century.

CHAPTER 7

SHAMANS IN THE RAINFOREST

The vast expanses of Amazon rainforest contain a seemingly infinite variety of indigenous Amerindian societies, each with its own variation in culture and belief but all sharing a 'magical' world-view in which sorcery is a potent and ever-present threat. Small in size, loose in social organisation and diverse in outlook, the present-day inhabitants of the jungle appear to have little in common with their illustrious ancestors who created Pre-Columbian America's greatest civilisations. This initial impression is strengthened by the fact that, contrary to popular belief, the rainforests of South America never developed high civilisation. Unlike the jungles of Mexico and Guatemala in central America, the Amazon forest conceals no lost cities, no baroque temples or imposing pyramids, and no forgotten treasures of gold or silver. These forest dwellers appear always to have been tribal—just as they are, in ever decreasing numbers, today.

In the wake of the Spanish conquest of Inca Peru in 1532, many expeditions, seduced by the lure of the *El Dorado* legend, set out in search of 'Golden Cities' which their native informants, eager for their conquerors to move on, assured them were always just over the next mountain range or deep in the heart of the Amazon basin. There were, however, no such cities, golden or otherwise, and there never had been.

The barrenness of the Amazon from the point of view of European delusions of lost treasure is, however, only part of the story, masking as it does significant facts relating to the origins of civilisation. For the everyday life of the inhabitants of the jungle, and the myths, legends and religious beliefs which serve to integrate them with their surroundings, stem, as one would expect, from the environment itself and the constraints which it imposes on human societies.

The Shaman as Sorcerer

Among the small tribal societies which still live in the Amazon basin, the shifting, transient way of life means that there is little need or scope for a hierarchical social organisation. The jungle's indigenous inhabitants are characterised by a simple but sufficient level of social, economic, political and religious specialisation. They cannot afford, nor do they require, a coterie of working priests, agricultural labourers or politicians—in other words, they cut their cultural cloth according to their social needs. Throughout most of the region the only prestigious public role is that of sorcerer or shaman—often referred to as the witch-doctor or medicine man.

By virtue of the nature of such societies, the shaman has to combine duties which, in larger civilisations, are assigned to priests, politicians, war leaders, doctors and historians. Shamans do not necessarily inherit their positions nor do they claim to be formally elected by their village or tribe, although this is implicit in the process of initiation. Instead, their power rests on their ability to claim convincingly that they have the support of the supernatural spirit realm. In the Amerindian jungle-world, the spheres of earth, sky and water, of times past, present and future, are all intricately entwined, controlled by ambivalent spirits and ancestors.

Only the shaman has the supernatural ability to journey in 'magical flight' to the other world in order to converse with the all-powerful spirits, and so upon his shoulders lies the burden of making sense of life. It is the shaman who claims to be able to rationalise the irrational by controlling the dangerous forces of supernature. However, before he is accepted as a powerful bargainer on behalf of his earthbound people, he has to prove his ability and earn their respect.

The shaman must have access to and be able to control the dark and threatening beings which wander through the forest beyond the boundaries of the village. Acting as a 'supernatural game-keeper', he controls the fertility and availability of wild game, the chances of a successful hunt and the ritual purification of any cooked food. Wielding the power conferred upon him by the spirits, he can also act as a potent war leader, divining the best time and place to attack an enemy. However, one of his most important tasks is the sending and curing of magical illness which is perceived to be caused by the spirits themselves.

The Amazonian shaman, the magic he weaves and the supernatural power he wields, are believed to be real in a forest world perilously alive with the ambivalent and untamed denizens of nature.

The First Shaman

Although the words 'witch-doctor', 'medicine man' and 'sorcerer' have often been used to describe those individuals who have contact with the supernatural, the term 'shaman' is by far the most accurate and least misleading. Originating from a Siberian word *saman*, which was introduced to the West by seventeenth-century Russian traders, the term is believed to have possessed an almost universal definition in the varied Tungus languages of north-east Asia. According to the Russian ethnographer Shirokogoroff, an authority on Tungus language and culture, the shaman's body is a receptacle for the spirits which he both controls and incarnates within himself as the need arises. The term 'shaman' refers, then, to an individual who can 'master' spirits, bend them to his own purpose and introdce them at will into his own body.

Originating with the Tungus people, the term 'shaman', and by extension 'shamanism', being what the shaman actually does, is inextricably linked to the nature of Tungus society. For these people, as with the native inhabitants of the Americas, unrestrained or wandering spirits can pose a dangerous threat to man and have to be controlled.

Thus such terms as 'sorcerer', diviner', 'spirit-medium' and 'witch-doctor' are evocative but not as accurate as 'shaman'. Shamans and shamanising are not confined to the tribal societies of north-east Asia and the Americas. Wherever hunting and gathering peoples exist there is usually a pervading belief in the spirit-world and a particular individual who is believed to be able to control it. Whilst such individuals are not always referred to as shamans, this is usually what they are. Shamans can be found in Africa, Asia, Australia, Oceania and, in ancient times, Europe as well.

As far as definitions go, the shaman in his guise as sorcerer is far more powerful, dangerous and inventive than a simple spirit-medium. Whilst the latter is merely possessed by spirits, the former is able to control them by virtue of conjuring them up, converting them to his point of view and then sending them away. The native peoples of the Amazon believe that their shamans control the spirits which themselves control the everyday affairs of man. As a result of his power, the shaman is regarded as a person of considerable physical and intellectual qualities whose soul embodies the essence of the tribe's identity.

The focal point of the shaman's activities, and the main occasion for the demonstration of his spirit-derived power, is the trance or séance, often narcotically induced, during which he interprets the myths, symbolism and magical reasoning of his society through storytelling, dramatic gestures and the chanting of magical songs. He relives the myths of the ages—myths which relate to the creation of the world, the continued existence of ancestors and the accepted ordering of the universe.

The shaman either knows more myths than anyone else or is able to interpret them more meaningfully; his influence and standing in society in part depend on this mastery. Thus he reveals himself as more than just a magician, mystic or medicine man, because he is actively engaged in manipulating, elaborating and reinforcing the existential fabric of society. He is a mediator between the natural and supernatural worlds, and by controlling the spirits he interprets 'culture'. A shaman cannot exist without his society, and a society without a shaman is in mortal danger of losing its identity.

A World of Spirits

To understand the rôle and influence of the shaman in Amerindian societies, the world-view within which he operates has also to be appreciated. This is all the more important because the native view of life differs so greatly from our own. The shaman, whether acting as a curer, ritual specialist, judge or supernatural warrior, is in effect binding his society together.

For Amerindians there exists no strict dividing line between what we term

Yanomamö hunter and family. *Photo, Steve Bowles, reproduced by permission*

the sacred and the profane, the natural and the supernatural, or between life and death. Whatever occurs in the physical world, whether it be illness, hunting success or good or bad luck, is seen as the result of spirit action 'out there' in the untamed jungle. Nothing in life happens accidentally: everything possesses either a spirit-cause or spirit-consequence.

Because everyday life does not run smoothly, there are always situations where shamans can claim an imbalance in the spirit world. The potential causes are legion—food or sex taboos may have been broken, evil or malicious thoughts may have been transmitted from one person to another, or someone may have neglected to act in a respectful way to a particular spirit. As a result, spirits may feel offended and vent their anger by sending illness or bad luck to the individual concerned. In such situations only the shaman, in magical séance, is able to journey to the celestial sphere to intercede with the appropriate spirit on the sufferer's behalf. During his celestial sojourn, the spirits talk to the shaman and tell him of the offence, and upon his return to earth he will suggest to the offender (or patient) what steps he or she should take. In this way the balance of the spirit world is regained and order and health return to the earthly world. In a universe of this kind, the shaman possesses something approaching a monopoly of spiritual and hence real (that is, social) power.

In order to accomplish his difficult and dangerous duties the shaman must, in effect, become what is called a 'Master of Thresholds'. He must be able to integrate different planes of existence and experience; he must be able to understand the nature of, and traverse the boundaries between, body and spirit, individual and village, natural and supernatural phenomena, and times present and past. It is his sacred duty to guarantee that his people conform to and are in tune with the established cosmic order as laid down in myth by the ancestors. This vital order continues to exist partly by virtue of the shaman crossing and re-crossing the boundaries which separate the natural and supernatural levels of experience. These two levels or worlds, whilst distinct, may be considered as connected aspects of reality, and the shaman links the two as a human bridge, by reliving the myths during his ritual séances.

Becoming a Master of Thresholds means achieving and maintaining a spiritual balance both within himself and within the spirit and earthly worlds. The North American Oglala Sioux shaman Black Elk, standing on a high mountain peak, said: '. . . I was seeing in a sacred manner, the shapes of things in the spirit, and the shape of all things as they must live together like one being.' Shamanism is therefore an integral part of what we may term an 'alternative' or holistic view of the world—a view where everything affects everything else and where the spirits of the dead exercise a pervasive influence on the conduct of the living.

The Ambiguous Personality

The shaman's role within society is by its very nature ambiguous. Balancing the past with the present, the living with the dead and the material with the spiritual, is not the everyday experience of ordinary people. Such ambiguities, it can be argued, may affect the shaman's personality to the extent that his ordinary behaviour exhibits ambiguities which we would term psychotic, paranoid or schizophrenic.

Ambiguity may take a variety of forms—some shamans, indeed, are sexually ambiguous. Amongst the North American Indians the *Berdache*, whilst physically a man, wears women's clothing and may, on occasion, affect female mannerisms to the point of simulating menstruation. The behaviour of the Berdache may in some instances be seen as homosexual, as he may even marry another man. However, the main point of this ambiguous personality and behaviour is that androgyny is seen as a visible union of obviously opposing characteristics—in this case male and female—which is an essential feature of the shaman.

South American shamans today do not appear to possess Berdache-like characteristics, but the female essence does play an important rôle. Among the Barasana Indians of the Colombian Amazon, Romi Kumu, a woman, is regarded in myth as having been the First Shaman, and from her all subsequent Barasana shamans derived their supernatural power and abilities. Romi Kumu herself was sexually ambiguous, as in many ways, the Barasana say, she was like a man. The ambiguity of that most obvious and definite feature of human life, sexual identity, is a prime tool for the shaman, who must proclaim his unusual status in a highly visible and understandable fashion.

The peculiar nature of the shaman has also been explained by recourse to the individual's psychological state of mind. Some aspects of his behaviour are said to resemble acute schizophrenia with the shamanic vocation often implying a crisis so deep that it sometimes borders on madness. Since an initiate cannot become a shaman until he has resolved this crisis, it plays the rôle of a mystical initiation.

This point of view argues that the internal stresses a shaman undergoes during his initiation and subsequent duties create abnormal attitudes and behaviour that in some situations appears to an outsider as schizophrenia. This interpretation, however, is not universally accepted; in any given society we must ask what is or is not 'abnormal'—do Amerindians themselves use the same definitions and labels as we do? The shaman's unique rôle means that he is given some leeway to act in an unusual fashion, which is part and parcel of his special ability to converse with the dangerous world of spirits. What may be considered unusual or even unacceptable behaviour by an ordinary person may be precisely what is regarded as 'normal' for the unique rôle of the shaman.

Shamans, by virtue of their social rôle, exist both within and without the boundaries of society. Their ambiguous status allows them to accomplish what is either impossible or dangerous for ordinary people to attempt. Whatever dress, behaviour or mannerisms the shaman adopts to facilitate the accomplishment of his duties is, to a degree, up to him. A non-shaman who tries to contact the spirits may fall ill, or his soul may leave his body to wander

A Tukano shaman's stool from the Amazonian Río Vaupés region of Colombia. *Drawing, Pauline Stringfellow, after Reichel-Dolmatoff 1975. Fig. 62*

aimlessly through the jungle; this is attributed to the fact that he is not trained as a shaman, nor is he able to master the thresholds between material and spiritual life. Only the shaman can patrol the existential boundaries of his society, both as a member of it and as an outsider.

The Quest for Power

In order to possess and wield the dangerous power of a shaman, the individual must first obtain knowledge and demonstrate to his own society that he can use it effectively on their behalf. In other words, he must prove his mastery over the spirit world. It is the process of initiation that both confers and legitimises this power and elevates the would-be shaman to his exalted position: by this ceremony he acquires knowledge and techniques which enable him to 'die' and be 'reborn' at will. This ability to transcend the most fundamental of all physical states is deliberately impressive, and lies at the heart of the prestige enjoyed by such individuals.

The anthropologist Arnold Van Gennep described the various stages of a shaman's initiation thus: firstly, the initiate is mentally and physically exhausted, thus bringing him to an abnormally high state of sensitivity; then he falls asleep and 'dies'. This is followed by his soul or essence rising up into the sky and then descending to earth again. Finally he wakes up as a fully-fledged shaman.

The focal point of the initiatory process is the so-called transitional or 'liminal' period, during which the initiate suffers the ultimate state of ambiguity. He is neither living nor dead, neither shaman nor non-shaman, but rather a 'living dead man' caught in the no-man's land between recognised states of being. Only if he successfully completes this rigorous test is he believed to be able to control life and death and to pass back and forth between the realms of the living and the dead. Having suffered and survived the ultimate ambiguity himself, he is entrusted with 'dying' and being 'reborn' on behalf of others—his people and his village.

The ceremony surrounding initiation rites varies from society to society, although its essential purpose is the same—to confer dangerous supernatural

Trophy head from the Amazon. Such objects were believed to contain powerful supernatural forces which deflected evil, providing its 'owner' with the power of ancestral spirits. *Photo, Courtesy of the Trustees of the British Museum*

power on the shaman. The case of the Akawaio Indians of Guyana, meticulously studied by the Oxford anthropologist Audrey Butt, is one of the clearest and best documented cases of shamanic initiation.

The call to become a shaman may take a variety of forms. A relative may persuade a young man to become a shaman, the desire to contact a dead relative may spark an interest, or perhaps an individual has survived a serious illness. In the latter case illness is often seen as a kind of 'death', and anyone who has overcome this personal crisis is seen to have cured himself and so be well qualified to cure others.

The first stage of an Akawaio shaman's initiation sees him physically separated from his friends and relatives in the village; he is made to drink vast quantities of strong tobacco juice, take magic charms and sing secret and powerful 'spirit songs'. Only constant practice will make him a master of these techniques, and the test comes with his first public séance which will probably be a curing session. Such initiation may last from a few months to many years, although twelve months is an average period, with the initiate's teachers being either living shamans or, on occasion, the ghosts of dead ones.

The acquisition of this dangerous spirit-derived power begins with the initiate drinking a potent mixture of water and tree bark, whose spirits help him to rise more easily into the sky and facilitate the departure of his soul from his body—a necessary prerequisite for 'initiatory death'. Equally important is the spirit known as Kalawali, who serves as a 'spirit-ladder' along which the forest spirits can descend to enter the initiate's body, allowing the shaman's soul to return to his body after its magical 'soul flight' to the spirit world. The symbolism here is clear—the would-be shaman must master both these spirits if he is to effect a voluntary 'death' and 'rebirth'. He must be able to go and return.

Other jungle spirits are also important. Tobacco juice itself is obtained from a spirit and helps the initiate soul to 'fly', aided by the Kumalak Bird (the Swallow-tailed Kite), which acts as the shaman's chief spirit helper. The Kumalak Bird lifts the shaman's soul upwards and takes it on its celestial journey. In addition, the initiate must learn to sing special 'flight songs' which help his spirit to fly away from earth. All these spirits have but one objective—to enable the initiate to break loose from his earthly shackles and ascend to the spirit realm in the sky.

A final but nevertheless important part of the initiation is the ability to 'use the leaves'. For the Akawaio, the rustling of forest leaves is believed to represent the forest spirits blowing their 'magical breath', which possesses potent curative powers. After all the techniques have been duly mastered, the initiate is ready for the climax of his training—his first public séance.

At this crucial display a large number of friends and relatives are invited to the initiate's house, where the host proceeds to imbibe a considerable quantity of tobacco juice and falls into a drunken trance. Then the séance begins. His spirit flies off to the spirit world and, if he has not mastered the techniques well enough, may not be able to find its way back to the land of the living; if this happens, another shaman is called in to help. If the initiate is successful in calling back his own spirit from its celestial journey, he is judged to be no longer a pupil but a true shaman. However, only subsequent experience will earn him a reputation as a powerful shaman—one who deals with 'magical death' and survives.

Magical Curing

The Amerindian concept of illness and disease differs from our Western ideas, in that it regards illness as the result of the evil actions of malicious spirit beings; consequently, treating the physical disorder alone cannot effect a total cure. A broken leg or a stillborn child may be perceived as the physical manifestation of a deeper-rooted spiritual imbalance caused, perhaps, by very real social tensions and jealousies within the village or tribe. The shaman has to appeal directly to the spirit world and, by placating the offended spirit, restores the patient's health. The success of this approach is due in no small measure to what could be called unconscious psychotherapy, because the nature of many illnesses are seen as culturally and spiritually, rather than physiologically, determined.

The Makiritaré Indians of Venezuela believe that illness may be the result of the breaking of the tribe's moral or ethical code, and that only a full confession of one's sins, and gifts to the shaman, can effect a cure. The patient must also observe cultural taboos if he is to regain full health and vigour. Among the Ecuadorian Jívaro, illness can be caused by the spirit attack of a shaman. If this is the diagnosis, the village's own shaman has to undergo a spirit trance in order to help his compatriot. The shaman drinks a herbal tea called *natema*, whose narcotic properties allow him to 'see' or perceive the offending object which has become lodged in the patient's body—shot there by the evil shaman. Come nightfall, he summons his spirit helpers or *tsentsak*, sucks out the evil essence of the malignant objects, spits them onto the ground for all to see and may on occasion send them back to their owner.

The Cashinahua, an Indian tribe of south-eastern Peru, recognise two types of curers. The first is a herbalist who deals with simple maladies such as sleeplessness, nausea and skin infections, whilst the second, referred to as *huni mukaya*, is considered much more powerful and deals with what is called 'bitter medicine'. During his curing sessions, this more powerful shaman will snuff tobacco in order to gain entrance to the spirit world. He passes his hands over the patient's body and, upon 'seeing' the illness, will prescribe herbal remedies dispensed by his less powerful colleague. If the illness is especially serious, he may suck out the evil essence contained in the pathogenic objects in much the same way as the Jívaro shaman.

Many curing sessions are held after nightfall to ensure the maximum audience and an emotionally charged atmosphere. Together with others, the shaman will interrogate the patient to ascertain his or her movements and actions over the previous few days. This question-and-answer session provides him with useful background information, allowing him to discover something the patient has said or done which can be interpreted as having offended a particular spirit. Identifying the offending act is quickly followed by the shaman contacting that spirit on the patient's behalf. The Héta Indians of South America regarded the jaguar as their most powerful ally in such curing practices. For instance, to cure snake-bite, burnt jaguar skin was rubbed into the bite marks, and for stomach ache, jaguar paws were rubbed over the stomach. A more general Héta cure for sickness required the jaguar's claws to scratch the patient until he bled.

Among the Cubeo Indians of the north-west Amazon, the North American anthropologist Irving Goldman witnessed a magical curing session and has left a detailed account of it. A patient was brought to a shaman widely regarded as a powerful curer. The shaman added forest leaves and black spines to two waterfilled pots and then began to blow cigarette smoke over the patient's body, pausing occasionally to blow smoke, firstly towards the river and then in the direction of the forest. As he did this he shook a rattle decorated with brightly coloured parakeet feathers, and intermittently chanted magic spells. After a while he poured the water over the patient's head, taking care to scoop up some of the black spines which he had added to the pot. He pointed to the spines lying all around on the ground, proceeded to gather them up and deposited them at the forest's edge. He then repeated the process with the second pot of water, and the cure was deemed complete.

On this occasion, however, the patient did not recover and subsequently died. The shaman explained his apparent failure by saying that the quantity of black spines (that is, the evil essence) which had been lodged in the patient's body had been too great; he had done his best but the power of the shaman who had 'sent' the illness had been too strong. This curing session was cleverly handled by the shaman: seeing that the patient was seriously ill, he had gathered a larger than normal quantity of spines and so had a ready excuse when his magic failed.

As can be seen from this account, shamans not only cure illness but also cause it by sending pathogenic objects in the form of darts or spines. Whether a shaman is good or evil depends, of course, on who you are and in which village you happen to live. As illness can be seen as having a magical essence, there is a constant fear of sorcery in many Amerindian societies.

The supernatural attack of a shaman can take various and dramatic forms: a warning is often sent in the shape of a nightmare, and then dangerous objects, such as black spines, can be 'shot' across large distances to lodge themselves in the person's body. Shamans can also cause illness or misfortune by acquiring the nail pairings, hair or dead skin of the intended victim, mixing it with various herbs and boiling the whole concoction; this produces severe stomach cramps in the victim. If a more serious injury is required, the brew can be kept boiling for several days, aided by the singing and chanting of the shaman, with the victim suffering severe attacks of vomiting. The *coup de grâce* can be delivered by the shaman breaking the pot containing the sickness-inducing mixture, which

A Tukano malocca or long-house, painted in charcoal and clay. *Photo, Brian Moser/Donald Tayler Collection, The Hutchinson Library*

by now is believed to contain the very soul of the victim; the unfortunate individual then dies.

There are further elaborations and different methods by which shamans may kill 'at a distance', such as sending 'death dreams', using plant poisons and blowing tobacco smoke in confined spaces. All these make use of the shared world-view of forest Indians—the pervading belief in the spirit world and the knowledge that only the shaman is able to control the spirits for good or evil. For these reasons, shamans are both feared and respected.

The Spirit of Politics

The shaman's unique skills give him power far beyond what we would term the simple curing of illness: his magical influence reaches out into the sphere of politics. Politicians are manipulators of social, economic and religious circumstance and the shaman, by virtue of controlling the spirits, can effectively manipulate the mechanism which is believed to produce the conditions of life. He can thus be seen to be wielding spirit-derived political power. He protects his village, tends to the health and well-being of its members and maintains it as a viable political unit.

Among the Kuikuru Indians of Brasil's Upper Xingú region, the shaman is recognised as exercising such crucial political control. In Kuikuru society formal political leadership is weak, and family life is notoriously unstable, with groups of relatives often moving house. In such situations it is the fear of the supernatural and of sorcery which acts as a method of social and political control. The faith which the Kuikuru have in their shaman allows him to pass judgements and suggest punishments without provoking resentment, since he is seen as merely relaying the wishes of the spirit world.

The anthropologist Gertrude Dole, who studied the Kuikuru in great depth, noted the following case illustrating the political aspect of the shaman's role. A house in the village had burnt down and the shaman, called Metsé, had to divine, through supernatural means, the identity of the guilty party. After interrogating the villagers and identifying a consensus opinion, Metsé came to a verdict which he knew everybody would accept: strangers had shot fire arrows into the house—the exact explanation proffered by the villagers themselves.

By their very nature shamans are inventive, often elaborating upon received opinions, and Metsé was no exception. He added that in the first instance these strangers had attempted to burn down his own house but had failed. In this way he made himself the prime target and put his own well-being at the forefront of his village's defence. The inference was that whoever had fired the arrows was really striking not at the unfortunate individual whose house had burnt down, but at the heart and soul of the village—in other words, Metsé, their shaman.

In order to put such events into perspective it must be remembered that Amazonian villages today are invariably quite small. In many areas a village may number no more than thirty individuals, and so social life takes place in close-knit communities where social tensions, perhaps arising out of keenly-felt jealousies and envy, can prove seriously disruptive. Individual relationships may easily spill over into the wider realm, creating social friction and, if not checked, political upheaval. The shaman's spirit power is the only force which can deal with the myriad initially trivial but potentially serious problems arising out of everyday life. In the egalitarian societies of the forest, mediation is the key to harmonious social relationships and the shaman is the mediator *par excellence*, for he intercedes not only between individuals but between individuals and spirits.

The Shaman's Judgement

Not surprisingly, a corollary of the shaman's political role is his judicial one. If, through political action, the shaman preserves the integrity of his society, then he must also be fulfilling at least some quasi-judicial obligations to his village: 'Shamans also had a hand in the administration of justice, for whatever misfortunes or deaths were attributed to witchcraft, the shaman was called upon to unmask the sorcerer.'

A good example of this is the disappearance of rice in an Akawaio village. Two villagers were apparently stealing rice for themselves without sharing it amongst their fellows. One of the thieves subsequently fell ill and the shaman was summoned to divine the cause of the illness. During his séance the spirits, using the shaman as their vehicle, warned the patient to avoid eating too much rice. This embarrassingly public diagnosis and verdict had the desired effect, and the patient soon returned the rice.

The main point here is that the illness was seen to result from the patient's misdemeanour in stealing the rice in the first place, but also, and more importantly, not sharing it out amongst his fellows. The situation was resolved without any direct social confrontation, as it was the spirits and not another individual who made the pronouncement and threatened consequences. This had the effect of publicly upholding the tenet that stealing was wrong. By placing the inquiry at the spirit level the personal element was removed, balance was restored and the shaman could be congratulated on having executed a masterpiece of tact and diplomacy.

Shamans, then, are much more than mere witch-doctors and sorcerers: they operate with equal ease in areas which we would term social, legal, medical and political. The interconnected nature of the Amerindian world-view makes them the supreme mediators and controllers of life. They remember the myths of the tribe, they interpret these for the benefit of their society, they see into the past as well as the future and are the guardians of the Amerindian world-view which itself creates and maintains a belief in their own abilities. However, in the art styles of such civilisations as the Olmec and Chavín, we are confronted with the image of the shaman as the jaguar, and it is to this supernatural association that we now turn.

CHAPTER 8

SHAMANS AND JAGUARS

Shamans are the acknowledged experts in contacting and controlling the ambivalent spirit world. Their power is at its peak during the emotionally charged séances and the way in which they may enter trance is of great interest and significance.

The Narcotic Dream World

Shamanic trance is often induced by the ritual use of narcotic drugs or hallucinogens, whose powerful effects disturb the brain's equilibrium and, in the view of Amerindians, set the soul free. Amerindian societies consider knowledge of hallucinogenic plants just a part of their intimate understanding of their natural environment, and their ritual use is an integral thread in the fabric of their life and culture.

This use of narcotics was first noted by Christopher Columbus, in a report of his second voyage of discovery between 1493 and 1496. The native habit of taking snuff was observed on the Caribbean island of Hispaniola, in that part now called Haiti. During a cult ritual, centring on the worship of carved wooden images called *cemis*, the devotees inhaled a narcotic snuff through wooden tubes inserted in their nostrils. Columbus noted that the 'Indians' accompanied this act by chanting incomprehensibly and then going out of their minds as if wildly intoxicated. This hallucinogenic agent of trance was called *cohoba* by the inhabitants and has subsequently been identified as *Anadenanthera peregrina*, a mimosa-like tree that grows up to 20 metres in height. The use of cohoba is widespread throughout the adjacent mainland of South America, to aid shamans in their ritual flights of ecstasy.

Although cohoba was the first indigenous narcotic to be observed by Europeans, it was by no means the only one. Among both the Pre-Columbian and modern indigenous inhabitants of the Americas, the knowledge and use of sacred plants was a vital part of spiritual and physical life. The coca leaf (*Erythroxylon coca*) played an important rôle in the public and private ceremonies of the Incas and their predecessors.

Coca was burnt in the temples by priests to divine the future, it was interred with the bodies of the dead, used to alleviate pain and to fortify the armies and official messengers or *chasqui*. Often referred to as the 'Divine Plant of the Incas', and as such strictly controlled by the Inca elite, it is more likely that by virtue of being widely used in pre-Inca times, coca was readily available for a variety of uses during the Inca period itself. Today, in the Andean heartland of what was the Inca empire, the coca leaf is still important in religious and social life. Chewing the leaf allays the pangs of hunger and fatigue, and an elaborate etiquette surrounds its consumption in an array of gestures, courtesies and offerings to Mother Earth. In Indian markets throughout Peru and Bolivia coca is openly sold, traded and bartered between the local inhabitants.

The Aztecs, similarly, used a variety of narcotic plants both for medicinal and magical purposes. Historical sources, written at the time of the conquest and subsequently, often attack what their Spanish authors—imbued with a sense of religious zealotry—viewed as the 'tools of the devil', the vehicles for communion with demons. The most famous were the cactus-like peyote (*Lophophora williamsii*), the seeds of the Morning Glory plant (*Rivea corymbosa*), referred to by the Aztecs as *ololiuhqui*, and the variety of so-called 'magic mushrooms', called *teonanacatl* or 'flesh of the gods'.

The *teonanacatl* mushrooms, usually identified as belonging to the species *Psilocybe*, appear in the Aztec codices, and during the 1950s it was discovered that in the Mexican state of Oaxaca, the Mazatec Indian curer Maria Sabina was still using these fungi to divine the causes of and cures for illness. Peyote, described as a veritable 'factory of alkaloids', is a powerful hallucinogen and comes from northern Mexico where it is still an integral part of the spiritual life of the Huichol Indians. Similarly, *ololiuhqui* was found in the late 1930s, again in Oaxaca, used in divinatory curing rites. Well known to the Aztecs, these three hallucinogens have to a greater or lesser degree survived the passage of centuries and the depredations of the Spanish. Along with other hallucinatory plants, their survival in indigenous ritual and belief represents a testament to the knowledge and respect which Amerindians have for these powerful plants and their ability to induce spectacular visions.

Vine of the Dead

Amongst the Ecuadorian Jívaro Indians of South America, as we have seen, shamans consume a narcotic tea called *natema*, which they say helps them to enter the supernatural world of Jívaro spirits. Variously known as *yagé* in Colombia, *caapi* in Brasil and *ayahuasca* in Peru, this powerful hallucinogen is prepared from the vine *Banisteriopsis caapi*. Jívaro shamans mix the plant juice with a variety of unidentified additives to make the intoxicating beverage, full of powerful alkaloids which induce a strong trance-like state similar to that of LSD.

The Jívaro shaman considers it of paramount importance to be able to carry out his curing duties in a structured and convincing fashion, and so stronger drugs, such as *maikuna* (*Datura arborea*)—which produces more powerful and uncontrollable hallucinations—are deliberately avoided. By virtue of deliver-

Indian market at Pisac near Cuzco, where coca is bartered and sold. *Photo, Author*

ing just the right amount of intoxification, *Banisteriopsis caapi* can be 'mastered' by many individuals who wish to regard themselves as shamans. According to the anthropologist Michael Harner, approximately one out of four Jívaro men can be considered as such, and as he himself says:

> Any adult, male or female, who desires to become such a practitioner, simply presents a gift to an already practising shaman, who administers the *Banisteriopsis* drink and gives some of his own supernatural power in the form of spirit-helpers, or *tsentsak*—to the apprentice.

For the Jívaro these *tsentsak* spirit-helpers possess both a natural and a supernatural aspect. The former is that of an ordinary object as seen without drinking *natema*. However, only by drinking the narcotic infusion can the 'real' supernatural aspect or 'essence' of the *tsentsak* be perceived in the variable forms of jaguars, monkeys and giant butterflies, whose function it is to aid the shaman in his other-worldly duties.

Harner has admitted that when he first began investigating the Jívaro in 1956, he did not fully appreciate the importance of this narcotic plant and the pivotal role it played in their ritual life. After experiencing the drug's effects at first hand, however, he relates how he entered a vivid dream-world, inhabited by dragon-like creatures and bird-headed people. Whilst it must be admitted that a Westerner cannot hope fully to comprehend either the full significance or the nuances of the Amerindian world-view as revealed in narcotic trance, such

Flanked by two jaguars with inlay eyes and teeth, this wooden bowl would have contained a powerful narcotic snuff, used by shamans to 'transform' into jaguars and hunt unwary souls in the mirror-image spirit realm. *Photo, Courtesy of the Trustees of the British Museum*

experiences do illustrate the ability of drugs like *ayahuasca* to profoundly alter states of consciousness, and hence perception.

Ayahuasca is used by shamans from many different tribal groups in north-west Amazonia, and its ritual consumption underlines the essential point that the Amerindian world-view unites the natural and supernatural in terms of separate but linked realities. The natural world is perceived in part as a reflection of the supernatural world, and only the shaman may with impunity cross the dangerous boundary between the two.

Accounts of the dramatic effects of *ayahuasca* are legion but can perhaps best be appreciated from an account given by Irving Goldman, an anthropologist who studied the Cubeo Indians of the Vaupes region of Colombia, where the drug is referred to as *mihi*.

> This sequence of *mihi* transports a man from vague and mild visions of whiteness to intense hallucinatory experiences, bursts of violence and finally loss of consciousness . . . At the beginning, the Indians say, the vision becomes blurred, things begin to look white, and one begins to lose the faculty of speech. The white visions turn to red. One Indian described it as a room spinning with feathers. This passes and one begins to see people in the bright colouring of the jaguar. When the final strong forms of *mihi* are taken the hallucinations begin to assume a disturbing and fearful form. One becomes aware of people milling about, shouting, weeping, threatening to kill. One is seized with fear that he no longer has a home. The houseposts and trees come alive and take the form of people. There is a strong sensation that an animal is biting one's buttocks, a feeling of the feet being tired. The earth spins and the ground rises to the head. There are moments of euphoria as well, when one hears music, the sound of people singing, and the sound of flowing water. The Cubeo do not take *mihi* for pleasure of its hallucinations but for the intensity of the total experience, for the wide sensation. I spoke to no one who pretended to enjoy it.

This graphic account of the effects of *ayahuasca* allows us momentarily to enter the Jívaro spirit world—alive with dream symbolism and the fantastical creations of the human mind. What we also come to realise is that these visions, whether they be brightly coloured jaguars or simple houseposts, are taken from the everyday world—in other words, the jungle and the village. A kaleidoscope of shifting images from real life is recalled by the brain under the influence of the drug, but perceived as if in a different dimension where physical shape, colour, size and sounds are all recombined in unfamiliar patterns.

To the Western mind the native inhabitants of the Amazon live in two worlds—the natural and the supernatural—but for the Indians themselves no such concrete distinction is made. The ritual use of hallucinogens reveals itself as firmly embedded in the culture and world-view of their societies, as an integral part of their vision of the universe and the complex web of beliefs which bind it and give it meaning. In such a universe men and animals can and do change their identity and appearance, slipping with apparent ease between one form and another. It comes as no surprise to find the shaman possessing an unrivalled ability to change his shape and form for magical purposes, for by so doing he is better able to master the spirits and protect his people.

Why Shamans are Jaguars

One of the shaman's most important duties is his ability to act as a 'Spirit Warrior', protecting the health, land, stability and identity of his village. His ability to converse with the spirit world is enhanced by his spirit-helpers, and one animal above all is identified with him—the carnivore at the top of the food chain, the predatory jaguar.

As we have seen, all creatures which appear to shamans during their narcotic visions are out-takes from the natural world. They may be bigger, more brightly coloured or more ferocious than their natural prototypes but they are identifiable as jaguars, caymans, eagles or snakes. The jaguar, by virtue of being the largest and most successful predator, can be seen as a natural choice for shamanic identification.

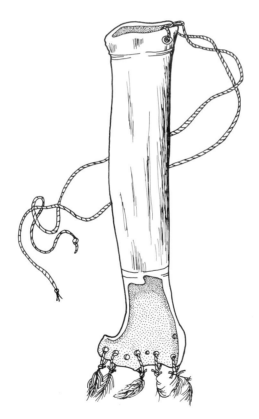

Narcotic snuff container carved out of a jaguar bone, from a Guahibo shaman's tool kit, north-west South America. *Drawing, Pauline Stringfellow, after Reichel-Dolmatoff 1975, Fig. 16*

That jaguars will attack and eat caymans is proof of their immense physical strength and endurance. Many accounts, reported by nineteenth- and twentieth-century explorers, relate how jaguars have been seen clawing the soft underbelly of the cayman, tapping the water with their tail to attract fish, hunting monkeys and birds in trees and attacking tapirs and giant ant-eaters on land. Equally at home therefore in water, on land and up trees, the jaguar is the hunter *par excellence*, impressive, beautiful, and above all resourceful. The natural behaviour of the jaguar parallels the supernatural behaviour of the shaman who is seen as a boundary crosser, able to travel in magical flight through the air, across the land and over water.

The idea of shaman-jaguar transformation is in some ways the Amerindian equivalent of the European phenomenon of the were-wolf. The currency of such European beliefs owed much to the prevailing religious climate and a form of collective hysteria; the ubiquity of reported sightings of were-wolves and witches was a social phenomenon based on jealousy, superstition and heightened expectations. In such a situation, otherwise patently absurd reports were taken seriously. Among native Amerindian societies, however, beliefs in animal-human transformation are not merely an episode in history but an all-pervading aspect of life.

During the seventeenth and eighteenth centuries the missionary activities of the Jesuits led to reports of the prevalence of a dramatic 'jaguar cult' amongst the Mojo Indians of eastern Bolivia. The Arawakan speaking natives regarded the jaguar as an awe-inspiring beast, and any hunter who survived its attack was seen as 'especially favoured', joining a group of powerful shamans called *camacoy*.

These jaguar-shamans were accorded considerable respect in Mojo society, receiving offerings of food and *chicha* beer from the villagers as payment for their supernatural protection when danger threatened. On such occasions the shaman would enter his hut to converse with the jaguar spirit, emerging some time later with torn and bloody clothes as if he had been clawed by the animal. If the villagers' offerings were not forthcoming, some sorcerers were believed to wreak their vengeance by themselves turning into jaguars.

The Mojo considered the killing of a jaguar a significant event and the successful hunter enjoyed great social prestige. At nightfall, during an elaborate ceremony, there would be a ritual eating of the animal's flesh accompanied by the rhythmic pounding of drums. The most potent elements of the dead jaguar, its skull and paws, were decorated with cotton and displayed in the tribe's great ceremonial house. The hunter himself would go into a place of seclusion, where the shaman would reveal the secret name of the jaguar which then became the hunter's own.

Many present-day Amerindians still believe in the supernatural power and essence of the jaguar and in its identification with the shaman. Among the Kogi of northern Colombia, the anthropologist Gerardo Reichel-Dolmatoff has reported myths and traditions which tell of great shamans who could turn themselves into jaguars at will. Kogi cosmogony is heavily laced with feline

The jaguar (Panthera onca), most feared predator of Central and South America, whose hunting prowess inspired Amerindian myth and Amazonian shamans. *Photo, Marion Morrison, South American Pictures*

Below left: The harpy eagle (Harpia harpyja) which inhabits the Amazon rainforest. Regarded by some Amazonian Indians as the 'jaguar of the skies', its features were often grafted onto feline representations by the Chavín artists. *Photo, Tony Morrison, South American Pictures*

Below right: The cayman, which inhabits the riverine environment of the Amazon river system and the old Olmec heartland. An important symbol, for both Olmec and Chavín artists, it was nevertheless subordinated to the jaguar. *Photo, Marion Morrison, South American Pictures*

A Tukano curing ceremony to commune with the spirits of the ancestors in the Men's House. *Photo, Brian Moser/ Donald Taylor collection, The Hutchinson Library*

Amazonian Xingú Indian ritual dance celebrated after the killing of a jaguar. *Photo, B. Leimbach, South American Pictures*

An echo of Pre-Columbian ritual in the Guerrero Village of Acatlán, Mexico. Two jaguar-men paw at each other, growling, as they warm up for a fight in honour of the jaguar deity who controls the rains. It is not uncommon for contestants to be knocked out. *Photo, Author*

symbolism: creation myths tell of a huge jaguar which was the first animal on earth, and of a fifth level of existence solely inhabited by jaguar-people. The Kogi themselves claim to be the 'sons of the jaguar', and they regard their society as containing the essence of the jaguar's supernatural qualities.

Shamans of the Guahibo tribe of the Venezuelan Llanos wear ceremonial headdresses decorated with jaguar claws and necklaces of jaguar teeth, and carry bags of jaguar fur in which they keep their magic stones, herbs and narcotic snuffing equipment. When a Guahibo shaman begins his magic trance, he paints his face with black spots to imitate the jaguar and transports his narcotic snuff powder in a hollow jaguar bone. The Sikuani, a sub-group of the Guahibo, dramatically sum up the importance and prevalence of the Amerindian belief in shaman-jaguar transformation thus: after snuffing large doses of the narcotic *Anandenanthera peregrina*, the men of the village dance and sing: 'We are jaguars, we are dancing like jaguars; our arrows are like the jaguar's fangs; we are fierce like jaguars.'

Among the Desana Indians of Colombia's Amazon, the shaman is also closely identified with the jaguar. The word for shaman in their language is *ye'e*, and this is also the term applied to the jaguar. Amongst the Desana the shaman is widely believed to be able to turn himself into a monstrous incarnation of this powerful feline. The objective of such shape-shifting is to enable the shaman to protect his own long-house or village, and to attack by supernatural means the

A Tukano Indian's box of ceremonial regalia showing a belt of jaguar teeth. *Photo, Brian Moser/Donald Tayler Collection, The Hutchinson Library*

enemies of his people or, on occasion, to hunt down the souls of unwary forest travellers.

A Desana shaman will adorn himself with various items of jaguar regalia in the belief that these highly visible associations will strengthen his magical bond with the beast and impart its fierceness and resourcefulness to him. To facilitate this dangerous transformation he will take a narcotic drug—not, in this case, the otherwise ubiquitous *ayahuasca*, but a hallucinogenic powder called *viho*, which we have already encountered in Haiti under the name of *cohoba*. After taking *viho*, Desana shamans will:

> . . . turn into jaguars and devour people . . . Having sneezed they continue to take the snuff. When doing this, and having fasted beforehand—they devour people. They use the jaguar costume. They do not move and lie there covered with ashes; only their hearts continue to beat while they are roaming at large in the shape of jaguars, to devour people. Thus they are roaming. Clad in their jaguar garments they turn up their faces . . . Once they have turned into jaguars they go and kill their enemies. When they devour people, all other jaguars become fierce too; very fierce they become.

This account shows that shaman-jaguar transformation and the eating of people all take place at the spirit level, under the narcotic influence of *viho*. The shaman's body stays still and in one place, but his predatory jaguar-soul or alter-ego wanders through the dark world of the jungle. Desana shamans are thus regarded as supernatural jaguar-beings only for as long as the *viho*-induced trance persists; as the drug wears off, so the shaman returns to the earthly world.

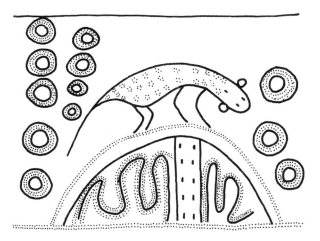

Hallucinatory image of the jaguar drawn by a Barasana Indian, from the Pira-paraná river of the Colombian Amazon. *Drawing, Pauline Stringfellow, after Reichel-Dolmatoff 1975. Fig. 57*

In searching for the significance of shaman-jaguar symbolism it is interesting to see how the shaman makes use of aspects of the real jaguar's behaviour in his nocturnal rituals. Religious beliefs and cultural traditions all have their origin in the complex interaction between people and their environment, and the case of the shaman-as-jaguar is no exception. However, parallels between what shamans do and what jaguars do is not necessarily a one-for-one imitation: only when aspects of jaguar behaviour are deemed relevant to the need at hand will the shaman borrow and adapt from his animal familiar.

At the onset of trance some shamans gather round and begin to utter a rapid panting sound, just as the real jaguar does whilst circling its victim. Some shamans will emit great roars in imitation of the jaguar, whilst others rub themselves with a plant whose smell is similar to that of the jaguar's odorous secretion when excited. By such imitations does the shaman more closely identify himself with the supreme jungle predator.

Even such obviously human and cultural traits as the use of narcotics may have a parallel in the animal kingdom. Although unproven, it has been suggested that jaguars may chew hallucinogenic vines which are often laced around the trunks of forest trees. This behaviour, if true, is obviously the animal acting in a natural way, perhaps using the vines as a purgative in much the same way as pet cats eat grass and catmint. It may also, however, have the effect of inducing unusual behaviour in the jaguar—behaviour that would have been observed by Amerindians and possibly imitated. Whilst such a theory is still speculation there is a parallel which suggests that humans do learn such habits from watching animals.

In the Tungus region of Russia, where shamanism was first documented and defined, the most powerful hallucinogen is the distinctive fly agaric mushroom (*Amanita muscaria*). The indigenous peoples of this area were famous for their reindeer hunting and herding, and it has been reported that these animals would often eat the hallucinogenic mushroom, lying down for hours under its powerful influence. This behaviour is cited as the origin of the human use of fly agaric in the rituals of shamanic trance, which have been well documented for the area.

The natural jaguar is a powerful predator whose appearance and behaviour, in the inventive hands of the shaman, is raw material for elaborating an infinitely malleable concept of man-animal and shaman-jaguar transformation. Differences in age, knowledge and pre-disposition mean that the jaguar concept may be interpreted differently by individuals and tribes. According to Reichel-Dolmatoff, the Desana Indians themselves possess at least three different interpretations of jaguar symbolism: some say that the 'were-jaguar' is simply a human who has been snuffing *viho*; others take the identification of the shaman with the jaguar at face value, by saying that a man merely puts on a jaguar skin; whilst others proffer the opinion that the 'jaguar' is neither a skin nor a real jaguar, but an 'essence' or 'state of mind', which enforces the individual to act like a jaguar.

A Desana shaman may become a jaguar either literally or metaphorically, but above all he sees himself and is perceived by others as acting 'like a jaguar' in certain situations—of aggression, hunting and dominance over others. The more powerful the shaman, the more 'jaguar essence' he possesses and the more successful he is likely to be. Thus the central aspect of 'jaguarness' is revealed: as jaguars dominate the animals of the forest, so shamans dominate lesser humans in society; the human hunter preys on animals as the jaguar does, and human warriors defeat their enemies as the jaguar eats its prey. The image of the jaguar works on a number of levels: it is the symbol of bravery, power and success—in the jungle, therefore, it is applied to the shaman as the only individual who occupies such an exalted social position—but in more sophisticated civilisations it becomes the emblem of political and royal power, closely identifying the ruler with a prestige developed over thousands of years by countless shamans.

CHAPTER 9

SYMBOL OF ROYALTY
AND SACRIFICE

Today archaeology makes considerable use of the evidence from anthropology to flesh out the bare bones of the archaeological record and suggest new ways of looking at material retrieved from excavations. In areas such as Central and South Ameica, where there is still some continuity of indigenous population, language and belief, archaeology is able to make good use of additional information and insights from other disciplines to decode the nature and workings of Pre-Columbian civilisations. The image of the jaguar and all that it signifies cuts across the boundaries between the living and the dead, the real and the imaginary, and the European and Amerindian world-views. In the light of anthropology, the archaeological evidence seems to suggest that this potent image also spans the divide between the Pre-Columbian past and the post-conquest period.

It can surely be no coincidence that both the Olmec and Chavín civilisations appear at a time which marks the beginnings of pristine civilisation in Mexico and of great urban development in Andean Peru. As Michael Coe, the excavator of Olmec San Lorenzo, says, there is almost no real art style prior to the appearance of the Olmec around 1200 BC. The rise of civilisation in Mexico went hand in hand with the development of an ideology expressed through an official art style. Lying behind both factors was the emergence of a complex and hierarchical society which possessed the manpower, direction and motivation necessary to create civilisation, to elaborate a pantheon of gods and to represent the official myths of dynastic rulership through art. In the Amerindian world-view, religion, art, social and political realities and mechanisms were all closely interwoven. The power of supernatural gods in the celestial sphere was perceived to be the basis of political power on earth.

Similarly, in Peru the essential features of Chavín de Huántar's impressive architecture were characterised by religious images—manipulated by a ruling elite in such a way as to suggest a supernatural backing for the earthly social order. The impressive art styles which so dominate the archaeological evidence for both Olmec and Chavín served to express the ideology of each. At the centre was the image of the jaguar, whose real and imaginary power was, even by 1000 BC, an age-old tradition.

The key to creating a civilisation is control—over people, land and resources—which may in part depend on the perceived control of animals, weather, and fertility. The jaguar concept, elaborated over centuries if not millennia, included this vital notion of control and the social and religious mechanisms which effected it. As the jaguar controlled the non-human world, so dynasties and priesthoods controlled human societies. The jaguar was the almost universal symbol of power and success and its recurring image was motivated by the aims and needs of ancient America's first civilisations.

The art styles of the Olmec and Chavín include the monumental and the miniature. Free-standing stone sculptures, elaborate textiles and goldwork in Peru, and monumental stone heads and finely made jades in Mexico, speak of an art that is anything but primitive and a society anything but egalitarian. Whatever the medium, the ideological message remained the same and served the same ends. Large stone sculptures are found in sacred places that functioned as centres for religious ceremony, and which were supported by the communal efforts of a more or less dispersed rural population. In turn the rulers and their priesthood supported their populace by intervening with the gods and controlling the universe. At the heart of all this expertise, craftsmanship and political authority was the jaguar, sometimes represented naturalistically but more often in the form of composite figures blending feline and human features—the power of nature tamed by culture and the power of the gods wielded by men.

Whilst the art styles of both cultures deal with similar ideas, they do so in completely different ways. Whereas the Olmec style creates a monumental feeling, even in the smaller pieces, with the artist often leaving open spaces, the artisans of Chavín produced a denser style in which every space was filled with extra detail. The dates for the two cultures overlap, with the Olmec falling between about 1250 and 400 BC, and the newest dates for Chavín being in the region of 850 to 200 BC. There is no real evidence for any cultural contact, and the detail and execution of the major artistic motifs seem to support this view. In addition, as we have seen, both cultural areas had differing histories. The Olmec represented pristine civilisation in Mexico, but in Peru civilised life, as reflected in large coastal architectural complexes with monumental art, was at least two thousand years old by the time Chavín developed.

Both cultures developed art styles whose content harked back to a tribal life in the jungle, and both ended up as impressive temple centres supported by an agricultural hinterland, expressing a potent ideology through an equally potent and dramatic art style. Through their art the two civilisations portrayed the symbols of their institutions, attitudes and beliefs, but it is as well to remember that archaeology possesses only part of the evidence. The more subtle indications of what real life was like between 1200 and 200 BC in ancient America have to be built up by careful analogy from the more detailed and recent evidence of anthropology. Both civilisations, however, exercised a profound effect on the art styles of subsequent cultures in Mexico and Peru.

After the demise of the Olmec and Chavín, the torch of Pre-Columbian civilisation passed to a succession of other cultures, many of which possessed feline symbolism in their art styles, religious beliefs and mythologies. As civilisation became more complex and more distant in time from their hunting and gathering forebears, belief systems also changed. Central concepts and images, such as the jaguar, however, were apparently deemed too vital to abandon.

People of the Desert

In Peru a multitude of civilisations made use of the jaguar icon in the art which expressed their underlying beliefs. One of the most famous was the Mochica culture, which flourished in the Moche valley on Peru's north coast between *c.* 200 BC and AD 600. More than any other South American civilisation, the Mochica portrayed almost every aspect of their everyday and sacred life through their pottery. Effigy pots, painted jars with distinctive stirrup-spouts and a series of realistically modelled scenes, all combine to give archaeologists a unique insight into the life and death of the desert people.

The feline image is ubiquitous in Mochica art. Sometimes identified as the puma and ocelot but more frequently as the jaguar, such representations depict their subject both naturalistically and anthropomorphically. Identifying deities from pottery evidence is always a risky business, but several important pieces seem to portray an anthropomorphic god, complete with bared feline fangs and a jaguar head, placed within what has been called a radiating-sun headdress. Variation in the appearance and surroundings of this fanged deity has led to its identification as several distinct deities, but the central theme seems in many cases to be the same. Ideas concerning hunting, aggression and killing are often made artistically explicit by portraying this deity actively hunting deer or taking part in a mythological combat with fantastic sea-creatures. In many scenes he is accompanied by a small spotted feline, perhaps a jaguar cub or ocelot.

Some of the most intriguing representations of jaguars in Mochica ceramic art are the effigy pots, which portray a snarling jaguar or puma standing manlike behind a seated human, with its paws resting on the individual's shoulders. Often the human figure has one eye closed, possibly indicating blindness or ritual eye sacrifice, his hands tied behind his back and a rope coiled around his neck. Examples of this type are to be found in public and private collections in Cambridge, New York and Berlin. The problem confronting archaeologists is to know what they represent. Are the large, standing felines attacking the human figures, or are they perhaps protecting them as alter-egos, in the same way that the jaguar spirit protects the shaman in forest societies?

An analysis of Mochica pottery displaying feline symbolism has been made by Elizabeth Benson, a North American specialist in Pre-Columbian art. She has concluded that the majority of such pieces are associated with two distinct themes—those depicting prisoners of war and those associated with rituals surrounding the important coca leaf. Coca is mainly grown on the eastern slopes of the Andes, and it may be that the Mochica either traded across the

Mochica ceramic effigy showing a seated dignitary with a baby jaguar or ocelot on his lap.
Photo, Author

Andes for this sacred plant, or made pilgrimages to its forested plantations—also the abode of the jaguar. To the Mochica, inhabitants of the dry coastal desert, the eerie and mist-shrouded forests of the eastern Andes must have seemed like a world alive with unknown spirits. A link between the narcotic coca leaf and the feline is clearly hinted at by a beautiful golden coca-bag in the shape of a jaguar. Inside were kept the dried leaves of the coca plant, imbued perhaps with the supernatural power of the jaguar and used by priests in their rituals.

Many of the humans depicted in front of the threatening jaguar image on Mochica pottery may be prisoners of war. A militaristic society, the Mochica conquered the adjacent valleys of Peru's north coast, bringing back large numbers of captured warriors to their capital. The pottery illustrates long lines of unfortunate victims tied together by ropes around their necks, their distinctive hair-style being characteristic of prisoners of war. Although there is no direct evidence, it is possible that on their coca-gathering expeditions to the

Fourteen hammered gold feline faces, possibly Mochica, from the North coast of Peru. Holes in the ears indicate they may originally have been attached to a woven headband. *Photo, Courtesy of Dumbarton Oaks Research Library and Collections, Washington, D.C.*

selva, or even through trade, the Mochica obtained jaguar cubs, raising them to maturity on the coast and using them in ritual human sacrifice. One beautifully painted pot, currently in the Art Institute of Chicago, shows a large feline sitting in front of a small man who is typically blind in one eye and has his hands bound behind his back. The feline seems to be about to tear at the man's throat and blood appears to be trickling from his mouth. If the pottery evidence can be relied upon, then the Mochica may have regarded themselves as the 'people of the jaguar'—the dominant and therefore most successful culture on Peru's coast at the time.

Some 1,000 kilometres south of the Moche valley lies a unique expanse of desert, dominated archaeologically by the closely related cultures of Paracas and Nazca. The arid Paracas peninsula has yielded vast quantities of beautifully preserved textiles, many belonging to a people who held sway over the nearby river-valleys of Pisco, Ica and Chincha, between about 900 and 200 BC. The small town of Nazca, nestled close against the foothills of the Andes, lies some 150 kilometres farther south and is famous worldwide for its intriguing array of desert drawings and confusing palimpsest of straight lines and geometrical drawings and confusing palimpsest of straight lines and geometrical figures. It is commonly thought that .Paracas society developed into the Nazca culture some time between 200 BC and the time of Christ, flourishing until around AD 600.

The earliest period of the Paracas culture parallels the lifetime of the Chavín civilisation in the Andes to the north. Many of the impressive textiles exhibiting feline symbolism are executed in Chavín style, and may represent imports from the northern Andes or imitations by local craftsmen. The style of these textiles reproduces in cloth the finely carved details of felines and feline-bird sculptures from Chavín de Huántar itself. Pottery, on the other hand, is hybrid in its appearance, reflecting local adaptations of the feline motif. The central features, however, remain—feline masks with rounded eyes and protruding fangs. A particularly impressive ceramic bottle, currently in the Museum für Völkerkunde in Munich, shows a half-human, half-feline face with great crossed fangs and Chavín-like eyes.

By the end of the Paracas period depictions of felines had become completely independent of the Chavín style. Around 200 BC, when Paracas was in the process of becoming the Nazca culture, feline motifs had changed beyond recognition and have been labelled by some as 'cat demons', hybrids of ocelot and otter. In appearance Nazca cat deities are essentially human in form, with feline faces, tails and paws. Whiskers are prominent on both pottery and textile representations and may have had a special significance which eludes us. Of all the depictions of felines in Nazca art, none is as exquisite as the one, painted on cloth, which is preserved today in the Cleveland Museum of Art. Forming perhaps a temple wall-hanging or ceremonial mantle, the central figure of this fragmentary textile is a human, elaborately dressed, with feline mask and prominent whiskers, a curling tail with a severed human head at its tip, and cat paws for both hands and feet. The trophy-head on the tail is a significant motif,

Nazca ceramic in the shape of a feline head. *Photo, Author*

for the figure is seen clasping in one paw another severed head and in the other an obsidian tipped knife, indicating ritual head-hunting.

The taking of human heads to 'capture' the powerful essence of the victim's soul is a well-documented practice in South America. In recent times the Jívaro tribe of Ecuador used to cut off an adversary's head, peel off the skin and cure it until it became a shrunken head—full of protective supernatural power. This gruesome practice is also indicated for prehistoric times, and the association of the Nazca feline being with trophy heads fits well into the concept of hunting and warrior success that lay at the heart of jaguar symbolism. So far from the Amazon and so close to the Pacific, it may seem surprising that Nazca culture used the feline motif so freely. However, trans-Andean trade and communication was not a new development, and ideas, beliefs and concepts travelled, along with more basic goods such as food and the ritual narcotic coca plant. The feline may have been interpreted in a distinctive style, but its underlying association with water, warriors, blood and supernatural power was still a potent combination.

Puma Drums and Inca Royalty

High up in the snow-clad Peruvian Andes, the last and greatest of all South American cultures was the imperial Inca civilisation. Conquered for the Spanish by the conquistador Francisco Pizarro in 1532, the Inca empire was nevertheless built by indigenous Amerindians, sharing the same world-view as their less imperial predecessors, and like them, Inca beliefs, rituals and art style contained much that was concerned with the feline theme.

The dominant feline in the Andes was not the jaguar but the puma. However, the Amerindian concept of what jaguars represented was still closely associated with this mountain feline, as can be seen from a remark made by the Spanish chronicler Garcilaso de la Vega. During a hunting expedition in which Inca guides accompanied their Spanish masters, a puma which had taken refuge in a tree was killed. Upon cutting open the animal's belly they found that it was a pregnant female carrying two unborn cubs. Both had spotted pelts and it was remarked that by virtue of this the father had been a jaguar. In fact this is not true, as all puma cubs possess spots at birth, losing them before maturity. From the Amerindian point of view, however, the jaguar may have been regarded as the father or master of all cats.

In Inca times the puma was an important symbol of royalty, just as the jaguar had been in earlier civilisations. The ceremony of *Capac Raymi* was held at the Inca capital of Cuzco and coincided with the summer solstice in December. At this time the young noble youths received their badges of manhood and were introduced into adult Inca society. These markers of adulthood included earspools which could only be worn by the aristocracy, and puma heads complete with their own golden earspools. The ceremony was accompanied by men dressed as pumas, who played the four drums of the most important Inca deity—the Sun God Inti.

Puma symbolism, apart from its importance in the initiatory rituals of noble youth, is, as one might expect, also found in the context of aggression and warfare and is intricately bound up with the militaristic origins of the Inca state. The drums mentioned above were played by men dressed in puma skins, and the drums themselves were made of the same material, the resulting sound being referred to as the 'voice of the puma' or 'thunderclap'. The puma's 'roar', therefore, could be produced at will by pounding the puma drums.

When the drums were played on the borders of the empire the Inca puma roared, announcing the advent of war. The Inca state may have been conceived as great puma which bestrode the Andes, conquering lesser peoples. There is of course a link here between shamans dressed as jaguars, hunting or eating their enemies in small tribal societies, and the puma empire of the Incas successfully defeating their foes.

Just as the jaguar's role is buttressed by myth, so was the status of the puma reinforced by official Inca mythology concerning the origins of the state. Whilst the early history of the Incas is shrouded in a confusing mist of alternative and unreliable accounts, it does seem fairly certain that the spur to imperialism came when Cuzco was threatened by a powerful confederation of nearby tribes, known as the Chanca. At the time Cuzco was ruled by Inca Urco who, along with his father Viracocha, fled the city in the belief that it could not be successfully defended. Another of Viracocha's sons, Yupanqui, along with allies and his own followers, decided to resist. Yupanqui, as war leader or *sinchi*,

Ceremonial ceramic polychrome vessel from the pre-Inca city of Tiwanaku, Bolivia. It displays Puma features in which the fangs are prominent. *Photo, Tony Morrison, South American Pictures*

placed the skin of the puma on his head in the belief that, like that animal, he would be strong and successful in the struggle to come. In a series of hard-fought battles he defeated the Chanca, turning the Incas into the dominant military power in the Andes. In the wake of this unexpected victory Yupanqui was glorified as a puma and acclaimed emperor, taking the name *Pachacuti* or 'cataclysm', by which he is more commonly known.

Feline symbolism, as an indicator of royal status, military success and divinity, is thus firmly established in Inca myth, ritual and political organisation. The puma, however, was also closely associated with the Inca capital of Cuzco itself. If the Inca emperor was identified as the victorious puma, his empire was similarly regarded as the body politic of the feline. Although there is considerable dispute about how to interpret the records left by various Spanish chroniclers, some authorities believe that the very shape and form of Cuzco was that of a gigantic puma, with the great fortress of Sacsayhuaman as its head and the confluence of two rivers at the other end of the city being identified as *Pumachupa*, or the puma's tail. In that part of the city known as *Puma-curcu*, pumas were kept for ritual purposes, tied up in captivity until they had been tamed.

Puma symbolism extended beyond the imperial capital. In the Inca province of Pumallacta lay villages where pumas were worshipped and, according to some sources, sacrifices of human hearts and blood were made to this important feline spirit. Even today in the small village of Acomayo, south-east of Cuzco, men are fêted as puma hunters, puma masks are worn in ceremonial

Rock carving in the shape of a puma from the region of Pacariqtambo, near Cuzco. The region has a special relationship with the imperial capital and Inca origin myths. *Photo, Brian S. Bauer. Reproduced by permission*

dances and the flesh of the animal is eaten in the belief that its meat imparts the strength of the beast to the hunter.

Thrones of Power

In Mexico, too, the feline was considered important in the art and ideology of many great civilisations. Among the Classic Maya, who flourished in the tropical rainforests of the Yucatán between AD 300 and 900, and for whom we have a mass of archaeological information, the jaguar was a recurring motif. In the byzantine complexity of Maya religion and art, the jaguar image was often portrayed as a deity. As the great Mayanist J. Eric Thompson stated, the attributes of the jaguar god are a large jaguar ear with characteristic rosette markings, whiskers, fangs and round animal-like eyes.

The Maya had an elaborate hieroglyphic system which they used in part to develop a complex calendar—different combinations of names and numbers being assigned to particular days. The jaguar often wears the number 7, sometimes on his cheek, and is designated the god of the day *Akbal*, the seventh day in a series beginning with *Caban*. In the Maya language *Akbal* means 'night' or 'darkness', which may well correlate with the fact that the jaguar, with his light-sensitive mirrored eyes, is a superb nocturnal predator. In Maya art a rolled-up jaguar skin symbolises the starry night sky. Incidentally, whilst the Aztecs arrived in central Mexico some four hundred years after the demise of the Classic Maya, their equivalent day name to *Akbal* meant 'house', the patron of which was Tepeyollotli—a jaguar deity whose labyrinthine realm in the dark heart of the mountain was entered through caves.

For the Maya the jaguar was closely associated with notions of the under-world, dark places and the night sky. As all normal social activity occurs during daylight hours, the time of darkness is a time of dangerous sorcery and witchcraft. Among the Lacandon, a surviving Maya group, there is a myth which relates that the world will end when jaguars rise up and leave their underground kingdom to devour both the sun and the moon.

Jaguar symbolism was also intimately associated with concepts of rulership among the Classic Maya—indeed, the very covering of their thrones was the brightly coloured pelt of the jaguar, just as it may have been for the Olmec. The image of the jaguar represented political power and religious authority, and in his famous *Relación de las Cosas de Yucatán*, which deals with the beliefs of the later Postclassic Maya, Bishop Diego de Landa describes the nobles as wearing jaguar skins. That this custom evidently goes back to Classic Maya times is graphically illustrated in the superb multicoloured murals from Bonampak, a small Maya site ony discovered in 1946.

The murals of Bonampak were painted along the walls of three different rooms and depict scenes from Maya ritual life between the years AD 790 and 792. Whilst a detailed analysis of the paintings does not concern us here, it is thought that the events portrayed are concerned with the announcement and legitimisation of a royal heir to the Bonampak throne. In Room 2 we see scenes from Maya warfare and the subsequent ritual torture of prisoners of war. The victors—inluding the ruler and his lords—are elegantly attired in bright jaguar skins, signifying their royal status and, in this instance, victory.

At the site of Yaxchilán, two lintels portray Maya lords with jaguar helmets, and one also carries a weapon made of a jaguar's foreleg. Gloves made of jaguar paws are seen on Stela 8 at the Maya city of Seibal, and jaguar capes and tunics are commonly found on the stelae, ceramics and monuments of such famous Maya sites as Copán, Tikal and Palenque. As with the Mochica, many jaguars appear paired with humans—threateningly large and perhaps acting as the supernatural protector of particular dignitaries. Because the Maya were more sophisticated, however, the appearance of the jaguar could have a number of meanings. Jaguars as masters of the underworld could signify that the human partner was now dead and 'belonged to the jaguar god', that the individual was a member of a jaguar caste, that he was a valiant and brave warrior, or indeed all three.

The jaguar symbol is found in contexts of warfare, fertility and sacrifice. In recent years the picture of Maya society as a peaceful intellectual civilisation has been shattered, and evidence has accumulated which indicates that human sacrifice was a focal point of their ritual life. In many depictions of ceremonial activities a curious implement is carried by the main figure. Three-pronged blades can be seen in the startling portrayal of a jaguar impersonator on a lintel of Temple III at Tikal in Guatemala. These peculiar blades have recently been interpreted by Francis Robicsek as instruments designed to inflict wounds which imitate the flesh-ripping attack of the jaguar. It has been suggested that Maya heart sacrifice reached its climax with the victim's body being eaten by jaguars. If this interpretation is correct, the blades stand as metaphors for jaguar claws wielded by high-ranking Maya dignitaries, themselves elaborately dressed in jaguar regalia.

The intimate association of the jaguar with Maya rulership is highlighted by the use of its skin as a covering for the thrones occupied by Maya lords. In the Quiché Maya language the word for 'mat' is *pop* and 'jaguar' is *balam*; they are often used interchangeably. The privilege of sitting on either a woven mat or a jaguar-skin mat was reserved for those of high status, as can be seen on many brightly coloured ceramics where rulers are sitting cross-legged on elaborate thrones covered with jaguar pelts. This aristocratic use of jaguar skins can also be seen in the painted books or codices from other parts of Mexico.

In the Maya realm the very shape of the throne was often in the form of a jaguar, some of which were Janus figures possessing two heads. Examples can be seen in front of the impressive Palace of the Governor at the site of Uxmal in northern Yucatán, and at the entrance to the Eastern Court at Copán. At the sprawling and multi-period site of Chichén-Itzá in the centre of northern Yucatán, there are no less than four jaguar thrones belonging to the later florescence of Maya civilisation under the Toltecs. The most famous of these is the so-called 'Red Jaguar', discovered inside the great temple of Kukulkán, the Feathered Serpent—more commonly known today as the 'Castillo'. This

Inca polychrome jaguar kero (ceremonial goblet) from the Cuzco region of Peru. Note the shiny silver eyes and neckband. *Photo, Courtesy of the Museum of the American Indian, Heye Foundation, New York*

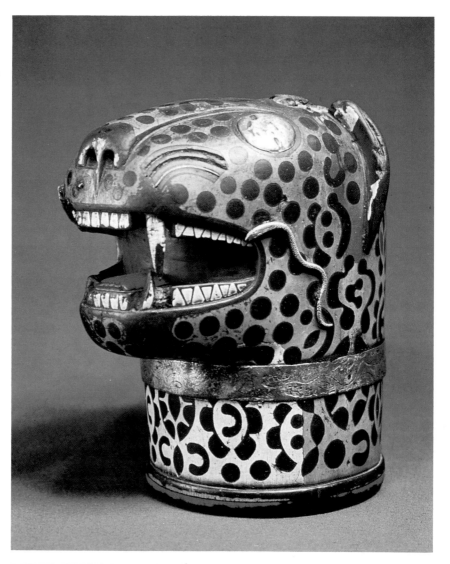

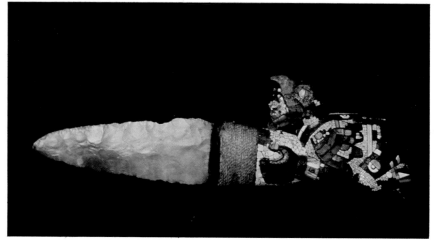

Sacrificial knife in Mixtec-Aztec style, with flint blade and turquoise mosaic handle, representing a crouching eagle warrior. *Photo, Courtesy of the Trustees of the British Museum*

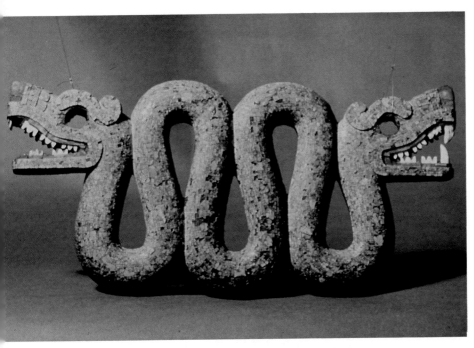

Aztec representation of the 'Feathered Serpent' (Quetzalcoatl), decorated with turquoise. The mouth and fangs suggest a jaguar character for this creature. *Photo, Courtesy of the Trustees of the British Museum*

Detail from the Aztec *Codex Magliabecchiano* showing elite jaguar knight fighting a sacrificial victim. The latter is armed with a feathered stick whilst the warrior's weapon is tipped with sharp obsidian. *Photo, Author*

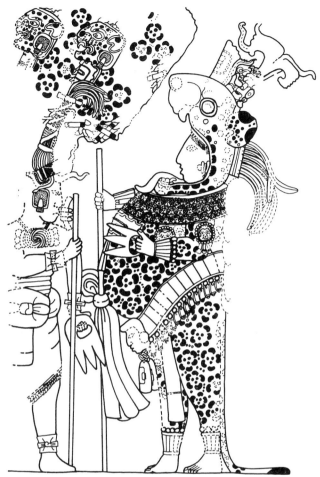

Classic Maya ruler dressed in elaborate jaguar suit and wielding a tri-pronged claw knife, carved on Lintel 2, Temple III at Tikal, Guatemala. Note the disembodied jaguar heads above the figures and the ruler's jaguar tail. *Drawing, Pauline Stringfellow, after W. R. Coe, Tikal Project, reproduced in The Ancient Maya, S. G. Morley, G. W. Brainerd and R. J. Sharer, Stanford University Press, 1983, Fig. 11, 20*

dramatic throne is rendered as a life-sized jaguar, brilliant red in colour and covered with some 73 jade discs imitating the rosette pattern of the real animal. In addition to these surviving examples, among the ceramic and sculptural remains there are many indications of the use of jaguar thrones from the Classic period.

A further indication of the importance of jaguar symbolism was the widespread use of jaguar names or titles as revealed in the hieroglyphic inscriptions. The particular jaguar glyph, identified by Maya specialists as T-751, is especially prevalent in the naming of the rulers of the city of Yaxchilán, situated in the heart of the Maya realm, along the Usumacinta river. Shield-Jaguar,

Lord Jaguar, Bird-Jaguar, Bat-Jaguar and Knotted-Eye Jaguar are examples of the profusion of names or titles which identified various Yaxchilán dignitaries. It appears to have been the practice amongst the Maya to send emissaries from one city to another, and on at least one occasion a jaguar emissary was sent from Yaxchilán to another city to attend ritual celebrations linked to the Maya calendar, and possibly for discussions concerning the matter of royal succession in an area over which the jaguar lords of Yaxchilán ruled.

During the height of its influence in the eighth century, Yaxchilán's great ruler, Bird-Jaguar, attended the funeral of a noblewoman from the nearby city of Altar de Sacrificios. A beautiful polychrome vase, found with the body of a young woman, depicts a scene from the funeral celebrations. Dated by its accompanying hieroglyphic inscription to AD 754, Bird-Jaguar is seen in a *danse macabre*, elaborately dressed in jaguar regalia, whilst a female relative of the deceased apparently commits ritual suicide with a large flint knife.

Polychrome Classic Maya vase from site of Altar de Sacrificios. The scene portrays the elaborate Maya ritual which accompanied the burial of a middle-aged noblewoman. Lower left, a young noblewoman is seen committing sacrifice with a flint knife. Above her, a dignitary from the city of Tikal wears jaguar regalia. In front of her is the eighth-century ruler of the nearby Maya city of Yaxchilán, engaged in a *danse macabre*. He is dressed in jaguar-skin trousers and gloves and wears an elaborate jaguar headdress. *Drawing, Pauline Stringfellow, after Henderson 1981, Fig. 50, pp 154–155*

Death and ritual bloodletting are closely associated with the jaguar during the Classic Maya period: often the basket which receives the blood offering is shown covered with dark spots, but whether these represent a basket covered with a jaguar skin, or simply the dark, coagulated blotches of dried human blood, is uncertain. There may, of course, be an interesting and significant conceptual link between the two.

Classic Maya politics were complicated affairs, involving an ever-changing scene of local alliances, marriages, military expeditions and ritual celebrations of astronomically determined and astrologically significant dates. On the basis of a detailed investigation by Joyce Marcus, an expert on Maya hieroglyphs, it seems that four Classic Maya cities—Yaxchilán, Palenque, Tikal and Calakmul—may have organised themselves into a military alliance, with the adoption of jaguar glyphs or titles marking the special status of the participating dynasties. For the Maya of the Classic Period the notions of aggressiveness and supernatural protection associated with the jaguar symbol permeated even the shifting political scene of the time. As the jaguar hunted in the jungle, so did Maya jaguar-rulers make war by preying on their neighbours.

With the carving of the last Long Count date in AD 909, the Classic Maya civilisation went into a dramatic decline, and by the middle of the century, for a number of different reasons, most of the cities in the southernmost part of the region were in ruins. But if the sun was setting on the baroque splendours of the Maya realm, it was rising on a new and militaristic era far to the north, in the central highlands of Mexico.

Warriors of the Jaguar Sun

The Aztecs are as maligned as they are famous. It was their fate to be flourishing at the time of Spanish conquest by Hernán Cortés, between 1519 and 1521, and, horrified at the evidence of human sacrifice which lay all around them, the Europeans wrote the chronicles and accounts of Aztec life and religion which form the basis of our present knowledge, and which are still the subject of controversy. It was not the Aztecs, however, who invented human sacrifice in the central plateau of the Mexican sierra. They partly inherited and partly assumed the mantle of a far more shadowy culture, known as the Toltecs, whose militaristic civilisation first produced the religious, ideological and political momentum so characteristic of this last Postclassic period of Mexican prehistory.

Toltec civilisation was short-lived, flourishing between the tenth and twelfth centuries. Their principal city was Tula, some 30 miles north of the present Mexico City, and chiefly famous today for its reconstructed temple-pyramid of Quetzalcóatl, the Plumed Serpent, with its four huge Atlantid statues. Otherwise, the ancient Toltec capital is not particularly impressive by Mexican standards.

Gruesome indications of Toltec rituals are to be found carved on a series of stone panels and free-standing stone sculptures. Originally all four sides of the

The four Atlantid statues on the Pyramid of Quetzalcóatl at Tula. *Photo, Author*

pyramid were probably covered with parallel rows of such carved and painted panels. Today only sections of the eastern and northern walls display such art, and their content is dramatic. Marching across the upper and lower registers are a series of jaguars and pumas or coyotes. Alternating rows depict crouching eagles tearing and eating the flesh of human hearts. It could be that these carnivorous animals were fed human hearts after the victim's sacrifice, or they may be metaphorical representations of Toltec warrior castes dedicated to the jaguar or the eagle. In other words, the Toltec warriors of the jaguar or eagle conquered and 'ate' their enemies, just as the real jaguar eats its prey.

Human sacrifice to the gods seems to have been part of Toltec ideology, intimately associated with the militaristic nature of the state. During this period a distinctive type of stone sculpture appeared—the *Chac Mool*—a reclining human figure with a tray placed in the centre of its chest. It has been suggested that such trays were receptacles for the bloody hearts ripped from the victims of war, but this is little more than speculation.

During the Postclassic era the earlier Mayan site of Chichén-Itzá underwent a renaissance at the hands of the Toltecs. There are many speculations as to how and why the Toltecs should have travelled right across Mexico to a foreign land and rejuvenated this city; whatever the reasons, the mark of the Toltec jaguar and its associations with the military orders and human sacrifice are graphically apparent in the sculpture which adorns the site's architecture. One

Toltec-Maya relief of a jaguar eating a (human ?) heart, from the 'Platform of the Eagles', Chichén-Itzá, Yucatán. *Drawing, Pauline Stringfellow*

of the most vivid representations is to be found on a gold disc recovered from the sacred well or *cenote*: it shows an elaborately dressed warrior, flanked by onlookers, cutting open the chest of a reclining victim.

At Chichén-Itzá the image of the jaguar is omnipresent. Monolithic feline carvings, called by archaeologists standard bearers, once snarled down from atop the stairways which led into the inner sanctum of the temple. The famous jaguar-thrones have already been described. In the central plaza of the city is the low-lying 'Platform of the Eagles and Jaguars', with decorated panels depicting superbly carved jaguars eating human hearts. Multi-block stone reliefs show warriors dressed in jaguar regalia flanked by human skulls, and even the ubiquitous stone heads, identified as Kukulkán, the feathered serpent, appear to have more than a little jaguar in them. The irony of Chichén-Itzá is that the Toltec elite, with the aid of Maya workmen, produced a more elaborate version of Toltec architecture in the Yucatán than they did in their own city of Tula. Jaguar symbolism, warrior societies and human sacrifice, however, remain the marker for the Toltec invasion of the region.

The Aztecs, or more accurately the *Mexica*, were Mexico's last Pre-Columbian civilisation. By virtue of their conquest by the Spanish, they straddle the boundary between the prehistoric and protohistoric periods. Their religion and their ideology of sacrifice are well expressed in their imperial art style—which blends motifs and ideas both from the past and from the various regions of Mexico which they conquered. Like their Toltec predecessors, with whom for political and dynastic reasons they associated themselves, the Aztecs were a militaristic society, freely mixing notions of conquest, tribute, world-view and human sacrifice.

As might be expected, the symbol of the jaguar is ominously present in Aztec art and ritual and is closely associated with war, sacrifice and royalty. Just as with the Classic Maya, notions of dynastic succession were heavily imbued with feline symbolism. At the coronation of the Aztec emperor Tizoc, the imperial throne was padded with jaguar skins and the obligatory rite of self-inflicted blood sacrifice was effected by piercing the skin with a pointed jaguar bone, fitted with a golden handle.

The link between the spilling of blood and the jaguar was also expressed by Nezahualpilli, the ruler of the royal city of Texcoco with which the Aztecs were closely linked by alliance. In a speech extolling the virtues of the imperial Aztec armies, he beseeches the populace to care for its brave and valiant soldiers, especially those belonging to the societies of the jaguar and eagle, who protect the realm and extend its boundaries by shedding their blood. If indeed these elite warriors formed the cutting edge of the Aztec armies, they could be seen as the bloody weapons of the state—their sharp obsidian spears and swords acting as the metaphorical teeth and claws of the jaguar. In place of the hunting jaguar, however, we have the predatory Aztec state engaged in conquering the diverse cultures of Postclassic Mexico in the years preceding the arrival of Europeans.

These Aztec warriors were so highly regarded that some authorities believe that the great mountain-top temple of Malinalco, west of Tenochtitlán, was dedicated solely to the military orders of the jaguar and eagle. Here the remains of monumental crouching jaguars flank a great stairway which leads to an inner sanctum dominated by a stone bench, into which the shapes of two eagles were carved either side of a jaguar. In another building at Malinalco are the remains of a mural depicting warriors, marching along what the Aztec art historian, Esther Pasztory, has interpreted as a path of jaguar spots.

An interesting perspective on the role of the jaguar and eagle warriors is provided by the evidence from the Great Aztec Temple or *El Templo Mayor*. Discovered in 1978 and excavated over the next four years, this sacred heart of the Aztec capital of Tenochtitlán has yielded a veritable treasure trove of Pre-Columbian art, and an impressive display of superimposed architecture. On the eastern flank of the great temple itself was uncovered a semi-subterranean temple dedicated to the eagle warriors. On either side of the stairway which gave access to the temple were two orange-coloured eagle heads, and on a lower level was a multicoloured ceremonial bench, depicting eagle warriors marching towards the sun. The presence of this temple, dedicated to an elite section of Aztec society, holds out the tantalising possibility that on the opposite flank, as yet unexcavated, there is a similar building dedicated to the jaguar warriors, exhibiting equally impressive feline sculptures and friezes.

In Aztec religion the jaguar was believed to control both the rains and lightning bolts. Where lightning struck the earth it was thought that there one would find blocks of jade—a kind of 'solid rain', green or blue and extremely precious. During the excavations at the Templo Mayor, an exquisite and complete skeleton of a jaguar was discovered, and between its fangs, enclosed

The coloured carved eagle head at the entrance to the temple of the eagle warriors at the Great Aztec Temple. *Photo, Author*

by its jaws, was a sacred green stone. It affords us a brief glimpse into the complex beliefs of the Aztecs, in which jaguars, jade, rain and fertility were all intimately associated. The practice of auto-sacrifice, during which the people would pierce their own skin to collect blood as a ritual offering to their gods, was often accomplished with 'spines' or lancets made of jade.

In the Aztec calendar there was a month dedicated to the jaguar, called *ocelotl* in the native Aztec language of Nahuatl. All those born under its sign were believed to possess the characteristics of this feline—they were courageous, daring and proud, and willing to fight for any good cause. On the first day of the Jaguar month, known as 'One Jaguar', there was a great feast for all born under that sign.

The calendar was punctuated by ceremonial festivities of a particularly gruesome kind, elaborately staged to impress not only the gods but the allies and enemies of the Aztec state. As part of the feast called *Tlacaxipehualiztli*, or 'the skinning of men', there was a ceremony called *Neteotoquiliztli*, in which sacrificial victims were dressed in costumes impersonating important deities. At its climax the victims were taken to a special courtyard and tied to a great stone of sacrifice or *temalacatl*. With the appearance of an old man dressed as a puma, warriors dressed as jaguars entered the arena, accompanied by music and chanting. Bound to the stone, forced to drink the sacred wine *teoctli*, and armed with a feathered stick, the unfortunate prisoners had to defend them-selves against an elite jaguar-knight armed with a shield and a wooden sword inset with sharp obsidian blades.

The jaguar-knight would cut and slash his bound opponent and, as the blood flowed, trumpets sounded, the prisoner was untied and led away to have his heart cut out by an obsidian knife and offered up to the Sun. In this instance the obsidian knife, rather than the sword, may have been a metaphor for jaguar teeth and claws. At least one of the containers which received the hearts for ritual burning, referred to as *cuauhxicalli*, was beautifully carved in the shape of a stone jaguar. The whole ceremony was intimately associated with the concept of fertility and was especially celebrated as a springtime ritual, with the jaguar warriors spilling the blood of men to the glory of the Aztec gods—petitioning, as it were, for their continued support.

Some authorities believe that the *Tlacaxipehualiztli* festival originated in the state of Guerrero. The chronicles indicate that this area was added to the Aztec empire around 1458, and as we shall see in the following chapter, it is precisely this area which has preserved the jaguar-man fertility dances and the dramatic blood-sacrifice rituals in such small rural villages as Acatlán and Zitlala. The conquest of such outlying areas may have materially affected the nature of the religious rituals held in the ancient island capital of Tenochtitlán.

Jaguar symbolism was the key to the identity of the supreme deity Tezcatlipoca, whose name means Lord of the Smoking Mirror. Amongst Amazonian societies the jaguar, with its shining eyes and connections with a reflected spirit-world, is closely associated with mirrors. To the Aztecs Tezcatlipoca was an omniscient being, the patron of royalty, and his magical mirror enabled him to see into the hearts or souls of men in much the same way as the shamans of the Amazon.

The carved stone jaguar *cuauhxicalli* or 'heart-container'. Discovered in 1901 in downtown Mexico City, it is a masterpiece of Aztec stone sculpture. *Photo, Author*

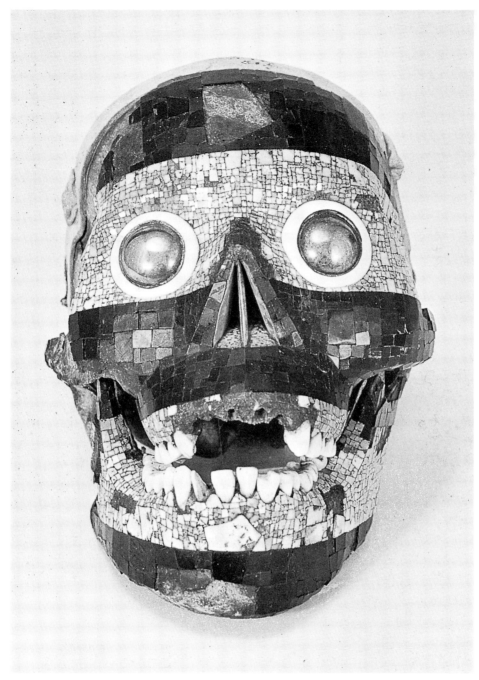

Aztec skull, decorated with jet and turquoise, representing the deity Tezcatlipoca, the 'Lord of the Smoking Mirror' whose shining eyes could see into the hearts of men. *Photo, Courtesy of the Trustees of the British Museum*

The link between blood sacrifice, jaguar warriors, royalty and Tezactlipoca is a fascinating one. Referred to as possessing shining eyes, this all-powerful deity had a manifestation as Tepeyollotli—the jaguar who lived in the heart of the mountain. Indeed, when the Spanish conquistadores first entered Tenochtitlán, the Aztec capital, they visited a temple in which stood a statue of Tezcatlipoca with a face like a jaguar's and bright, piercing eyes of shiny black obsidian. Volcanoes are mountains and it is from them that obsidian is mined. Used to manufacture the sacrificial knives and warrior sword-blades of the Aztecs, obsidian was a sacred as well as practical material. The word for obsidian in the Aztec language is *itztli*, and this was considered to be yet another manifestation of Tezcatlipoca.

Thus there would appear to be a conceptual link between the shaman as jaguar in tribal societies and Tezcatlipoca as jaguar in the Aztec pantheon. Cultures and civilisations may vary in their size and sophistication, but many of the underlying ideas, and the patterns of thought and association, remain. Even for the cultured and imperial Aztecs, the essence of 'jaguarness' was ever-present.

The symbol of the jaguar, and occasionally the puma, spans the millennia of Pre-Columbian civilisations. Military prowess, supernatural power and political success are intricately woven into a rich tapestry of beliefs and attitudes which reflect in part the ideologies of prehistoric civilisations. The jaguar was a symbol of royal authority, jaguar-knights led the Aztec armies into battle, Maya rulers, elaborately garbed in brightly coloured jaguar skins, practised gruesome rites of heart sacrifice, and the Mochica of Peru tied together the image of the jaguar and the rituals surrounding prisoners of war. For Pre-Columbian civilisations the image of the jaguar was indissolubly linked to notions of pre-eminence and dominance, and is reflected and preserved in their art.

Today there are still faint echoes of this fascination with the feline theme in the remoter parts of Central and South America. Sometimes the jaguar appears in an almost purely indigenous form, at other times freely mixed with Catholic symbolism. Cultural change continues apace, but the age-old beliefs in the power of felines and their supernatural associations with death and fertility continue to exercise a firm hold on the minds of America's native peoples, as it has done for at least three thousand years.

CHAPTER 10

THE ENDURING BELIEF

The shadow of the jaguar stalked ancient America in a manner difficult for us to comprehend. For those who lived in the Pre-Columbian world, as for many surviving indigenous societies, there were two jaguars—the real and the imaginary, the natural and the supernatural. The former developed over several million years of evolution; the latter was a creation of the human mind, sometimes under the influence of powerful narcotic drugs. Whilst distinct, the supernatural creature owed more than a little to its real counterpart—this beautiful, powerful cat which was, with the exception of man, the most successful predator in the Americas. Its claws, fangs and dramatic snarl were full of real and imagined danger, and its behaviour made it a model of hunting success and bravery to the tribal societies and great civilisations of the Americas.

The Power of Felines

Across the world and throughout history, animals have exercised a fascination for humans, finding their way into religious beliefs, mythology and art. Creatures as varied as the bear, serpent, eagle and horse occur time and again, playing a central rôle in the lives of many cultures. By far the most dramatic of such animals, however, are the felines. The winged lions of Assyria, the Sphinx of Egypt, the tiger deities and spirits of Asia—everywhere we find human societies integrating felines into the rich tapestry of their cultural life.

There appears to be something about large predatory felines which strikes an almost universal chord in the human imagination and which makes them suitable vehicles for expressing human qualities such as ferocity, bravery, power, danger and success. Notions of felines as competitors to humans probably have little to do with any direct confrontation. Few large cats eat humans, and when they do it is usually because they are wounded, disorientated, starving or have mistaken an unfortunate human for their natural prey. The competition between feline and human is based rather on the fact that carnivorous cats hunt and kill the same prey as man.

Humankind developed in Africa over several million years ago. As our hominid ancestors acquired new abilities, they gradually improved their chances of survival. At first, there were probably so few of them that competition between man and the successful carnivorous predators, such as lions and leopards, must have unequally favoured the latter. To survive, early man had to compete with them. Small numbers of our primitive ancestors developed language, social cohesion and tactics which enhanced the viability of their social group. Co-operative hunting may have been learned partly in imitation of the lion's tactics. This impressive feline, so successful in its predatory behaviour that it spends almost 20 hours a day sleeping, may have been one of the most potent images implanted into the developing brain of early man.

In ancient America, at a time before the rise of such civilisations as the Olmec or Chavín, most communities were hunters and gatherers, although some were developing agriculture. Between about 3000 BC and 1000 BC complex societies developed against an increasingly agricultural background which still had as its focus beliefs firmly locked into a hunting ethos. At a conservative estimate, man has been in the Americas since c. 11,000 BP and possibly much earlier; for all but the last three or four thousand years Amerindians lived in a hunting and gathering world, alive with spirits of the hunt— a true stone age existence in which powerful animals, as pre-eminent hunters, often played a prominent role.

In the harsh reality of the jungle, both the jaguar and human hunters sought to improve their hunting success. Both actively pursued the same prey, but the forest, then as now, was the natural abode of the jaguar, not man. Men had to leave the safety of the village in order to enter the jaguar's dangerous world of unknown spirits. In order to be successful the human hunter had to adopt both the jaguar's tactics and, in part, his identity.

Humans have no natural weapons to compare with those of their feline competitors. The jaguar, like all large cats, possesses great strength, excellent vision, agility, an acute sense of smell and a lethal armoury of sharp teeth, fangs and claws. Unarmed, a hunter could not hope to compete with, or defend himself against the jaguar. To compensate, he had to equip himself with spears, arrows and knives, and, as we have seen, amongst many Amerindian groups these weapons are regarded as analogues of the jaguar's teeth and claws. In essence, we can say that when in the jaguar's domain, human hunters have to become as like the animal as possible.

Like lions or tigers in other parts of the world, in the Americas it was the jaguar who assumed the 'royal mantle' as king of the beasts, and by equating their weapons with feline fangs and claws, human hunters may have hoped to match the jaguar's success. However, the notion of drawing parallels between hunting men and the jaguar goes beyond simply referring to one's spear-points as the 'teeth of the jaguar': such symbolism pervades the sphere of dress and ritual paraphernalia as well. Jaguar teeth and claws were commonly used as personal ornaments, in the belief that they endowed the wearer with the animal's attributes. Imitating the jaguar's roar, appearance and behaviour can be seen as psychologically closing the gap between animals and humans, and consequently allying humankind to the power of nature as expressed by nature's own most successful predator.

Aspects of the jaguar, like teeth and claws, are metaphors used by Amerindians in a subtle but understandable way. What they are really saying is that the hunter's knife or spear cuts the flesh, exactly as the jaguar's teeth and claws despatch its prey. This particular way of thinking can also be used to describe relations between people of different tribes. As a jaguar is the hunter *par excellence* of the forest prey, so fierce warriors are the supreme hunters of other humans. In other words, the victorious warrior who has defeated his enemy *is like* the jaguar who kills his prey, and the shaman, who in ritual trance defeats another shaman or a supernatural demon, is showing his superior power over that person or being. By virtue of hunting their prey, jaguars control them, and likewise shamans control the dangerous forces of supernature. Statements like 'That shaman is a jaguar' or 'Those warriors are jaguars' are meaningless on their own; only by understanding the context of such utterances can we make any sense of them. If, for example, one tribe raids and defeats another, taking its women and food, and killing its young men in battle, the losers may justly refer to 'those fierce people' as 'jaguars'.

The link between Amerindian ideals and the jaguar is made explicit in some indigenous languages where the word for predator is *yai*. This same name is applied to a bird which eats insects, the shaman who hunts the souls of lesser humans and the jaguar which kills tapirs, caymans and deer. All, from the point of view of the unfortunate victims, are predators. And as the jaguar is the most successful predator, and humans do the labelling, the word *yai* is most often used to describe the fierce behaviour of both. To 'be jaguar', therefore, is to be a successful hunter, whether of forest game or of people.

The power of jaguars possesses a magical quality, part real and part imaginary. Primeval fears, deeply ingrained in the human brain perhaps several million years ago, combined with the comnpulsive needs of men to understand their surroundings, has led, in the Americas, to the jaguar representing vital qualities in human society. The notions of success and prestige have spilled over into the realm of religious beliefs and their representation in art. Jaguar symbolism, portrayed in cave paintings, goldwork, pottery and stone sculpture, is therefore closely associated with supernatural deities and important individuals. The jaguar became the symbol of royalty, the expression of military dominance and political control, and of the vital supernatural support upon which such powers were believed to rest.

In consequence, jaguar symbolism became entwined with ideas concerning blood, rain, water and thus the whole concept of fertility. Such associations are still to be seen in both Central and South America and are closely linked to Amerindian beliefs regarding the nature of their cosmos. For example, amongst the contemporary Quechua peoples of the Peruvian and Bolivian Andes there exists a belief in a supernatural flying feline known as the Ccoa. The most feared and active spirit in the region, this creature is intimately associated with the everyday affairs of men. The Quechua say the Ccoa's roar is like thunder, that it sends lightning with its eyes, spits hail and urinates rain. Some authorities regard this supernatural cat as a sky-god which controls the elements and thus the fertility of crops and animals alike. By exercising such vital powers the Ccoa is also closely identified with those who practise magic and sorcery.

More commonly, the importance of the jaguar is seen in what have been called folk-festivals and folk-art, echoes of the past which nevertheless illustrate the animal's continuing pre-eminence, even in the latter part of the twentieth century.

Mask of the Jaguar

Dramatic and colourful masks still used in many Mexican folk festivals are a particularly good example of the way in which the image of the jaguar has

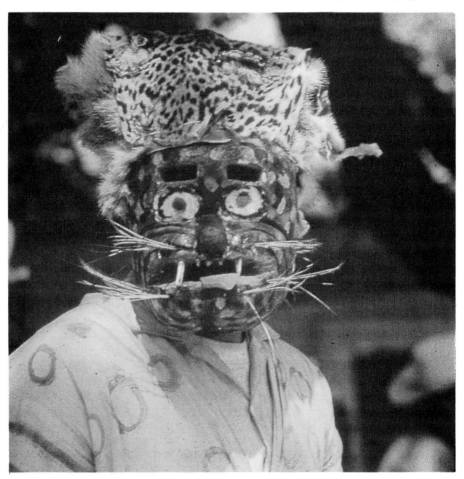

Jaguar-impersonator at the village of Tlapa, Guerrero, Mexico. *Photo, Marion Oettinger*

maintained its fascination. Whilst a variety of animals and human caricatures are found, nevertheless, as Donald Cordry, the famous collector and historian of Mexican masks, says, it is the jaguar which remains the most popular subject amongst modern mask-makers.

The purpose of any mask is to transform its wearer from an ordinary human to an extraordinary being, sometimes deliberately ambiguous and at other times representing a half-human, half-animal creature or deity. The festival or ritual during which a mask is worn is also a special occasion—a situation which is by definition extraordinary. Wearing a jaguar mask 'creates' a jaguar persona and enables the wearer to act out the cosmic or mythical role of the beast in a particular cultural setting. It is a sign of how deeply the jaguar concept is ingrained in the Mexican psyche that such masks remain so popular, despite the fact that today real jaguars are comparatively rare. Many modern mask-makers have probably never seen a real jaguar outside a zoo, although they may have observed the ocelot in the wild country of the sierra.

Most jaguar masks are referred to colloquially as *tigre* masks—an evident confusion which originated with the Spanish and Portuguese explorers who discovered and colonised the Americas during the late fifteenth and early sixteenth centuries. Observing large cats, such as the jaguar and puma, they referred to them as tigers and lions—a habit imitated by the local inhabitants who now refer to them as *tigre* and *león* respectively.

Jaguar masks are subject to a great variety of local interpretation and elaboration. Particular styles are often so distinctive that they can immediately be assigned to a certain region of Mexico, and sometimes to particular workshops or craftsmen. Those from Olinalá in Guerrero are famous—fashioned from wood, brightly coloured and covered in shiny lacquer. Masks such as these are used in a number of ceremonial 'jaguar dances'. At Zitlala and Acatlán, also in Guerrero, masks are more accurately described as *cascos* or helmets, made from toughened leather and painted yellow or green. These are designed to be worn as protective headgear in pugilistic displays of ritualised violence.

The yellow colour of most jaguar masks can be seen not simply as the natural colour of the real jaguar, but also as the colour of ripe maize, the ancient and modern staple food of Mexico. Jaguar dances, in which young men dress up in jaguar suits and wear jaguar masks or helmets, are held in the spring to encourage the jaguar deity to send rain, in an age-old belief that jaguars, rain and fertility are all part of the same concept. Such 'rain ceremonies' admit that the jaguar is the controller or bringer of rains.

Mirrors and Eyes

One of the most distinctive features of Mexican jaguar or *tigre* masks is that they often possess glittering, mirrored eyes, which seem to follow the observer wherever he or she goes. The use of mirrors as eyes is an unnerving practice, which seems to give the mask a life of its own and to strengthen the illusion that

Jaguar mask with whiskers, fangs and mirrored eyes, from Guerrero, Mexico. *Photo, Author*

the wearer has been somehow transformed into a new creature, combining animal, human and perhaps supernatural qualities.

The notion of mirrored eyes is an important aspect of the whole jaguar concept. As we have seen, Amerindians believe in the shadowy existence of parallel spirit worlds which are reflections of real life. Central to this belief is the notion that shamans can see the true nature of one's soul—a soul essence—by using mirrors. During their drug-induced séances, they often use mirrors to divine the future in their nocturnal rituals. The Tukano Indians of Colombia squeeze the juice from forest plants into their eyes to produce a strong dilation of the pupils, giving them what they call 'jaguar vision' and the ability to see in the dark. Other shamans believe they are transformed into jaguars when they put on a jaguar mask, which carries with it the power to perceive things not as humans but as jaguars.

In this context the jaguar becomes the 'Master of Game Animals' and is often regarded as the double of the shaman, both being referred to as *yai*; the jaguar is believed to control a mirror-image universe beneath the hills, where everything is organised as a reflection of human society. A person's shadow and watery reflection are both related to this parallel world, and only the shaman in trance can penetrate the boundary which separates the two universes. Amongst Amerindians mirrors are metaphors for 'eyes', but what they reveal is perceived as inherently dangerous because it is the very essence of life and death.

The link between the mirrored eyes of jaguar masks, real jaguars and Amerindian beliefs in a parallel spirit-world is a fascinating one. Real jaguars, like all cats, possess a dense layer of light-gathering cells at the back of the eye, called the *tapetum lucidum*. Whilst this enables them to see better in the dark and be more efficient predators, it also means that their eyes appear to glow in the dark when a light is placed in front of them. Both real jaguars and humans wearing jaguar masks seem to carry the image of light and fire in their glittering, reflective eyes. The biology of real jaguars appears to have had a profound effect on the mind of Amerindians, and their eyes have been incorporated into a whole set of beliefs concerning mirrors, mirror images and parallel spirit-worlds.

The magic mirror, as we have seen, was Tezcatlipoca's trademark, and may be regarded as a metaphor for human eyes because with it he was believed to be able to see into the very hearts of men. For the Aztecs this magical device emitted smoke, just as the warm earth releases a swirling mist after the cooling rains. Whilst Tezcatlipoca is a complex god, belonging to a large and sophisticated civilisation, his jaguar form, his 'all-seeing' mirrored eyes and his connections with rain and fertility, make him recognisably a product of the Amerindian fascination with the jaguar.

For the Aztecs, eyes signified rain and water, which in turn was a favourable augury for it meant a successful maize crop. Tears were thought to mimic rain, and in the ritual sacrifice of young children to Tlaloc, the rain god, it was thought to be good luck if the child cried during the preparations, for then the rains would surely come. Human sacrifice, along with many other vestiges of Pre-Columbian Mexican beliefs, have long since disappeared, but in the remoter parts of Mexico the descendants of the Aztecs still offer blood sacrifices directly to the jaguar deity, some 500 years after the Spanish conquest.

Village of the Jaguar

Acatlán is a small village locked away in the mountain recesses of the Mexican state of Guerrero. Its geographical isolation has enabled it to retain a fascinating 'Jaguar Festival' which combines centuries-old Aztec beliefs with a still more ancient set of beliefs concerning the jaguar.

Many small rural Mexican villages have festivals which include men dressing up as jaguars and being ceremonially 'hunted' in the form of entertaining dances—the communities of Totoltepec and Olinalá, for example.

Here young men dress up as jaguars and dance around the main square in the hope of precipitating the rains which will fertilise the young maize seedlings. In the small village of Zitlala young men don huge leather helmets with mirrored eyes, and whip each other with ropes until one contestant falls to the ground.

The festival at Acatlán, however, is dramatically different. Every spring, between 1st and 5th May, a bloody confrontation takes place between young men of the village, dressed in jaguar costumes, boxing gloves and protected by helmets made of toughened leather in the shape of a snarling jaguar face. Thus equipped, they engage in fierce fist fights with the objective of spilling each others' blood. For the inhabitants of Acatlán, human blood is considered analogous to rain: both are vital liquids and potent symbols of fertility.

The idea lying behind this highly structured festival is that the mountain-dwelling jaguar god, called by the Aztecs Tepeyollotli or 'Heart of the Mountain', is the 'Master of Rains' and by extension the controller of earthly fertility. Only by spilling their blood for the jaguar god will he in turn spill his blood in the form of rain to fertilise Acatlán's parched maize fields. The very survival of the village is seen to depend on the success of these jaguar fights.

Acatlán itself has about 1,500 inhabitants and was established as an Aztec colony by the emperor Motecuzhoma ·in the years just before the Spanish conquest of 1519–21. The sonorous tones of the Aztec language, Nahuatl, can be freely heard mingling with the harsher sounds of Spanish introduced by the conquistadores. The village relies primarily on agriculture, and maize is by far the most important crop. By the beginning of May the maize has been sown, the

Two jaguar-men from Acatlán, Guerrero, Mexico, running towards the sacred circle to prepare for the ritual fights in honour of the jaguar deity who controls the rains. One carries a branch tipped with blood-red flowers—an echo of Pre-Columbian Aztec practices where such symbolism honoured the all-seeing Aztec deity Tezcatlipoca, the 'Lord of the Smoking Mirror'.

earth is dry and social tension fills the air as everyone awaits the coming of the rains.

Whilst the festival begins in the village itself, the jaguar fights take place on top of a local mountain called *Cerro Azúl* or Blue Mountain—the very name possessing obvious links with rain, water and fertility. Cerro Azúl is about three hours' walk up from the village, and the whole event takes on the character of a sacred pilgrimage. Once at the summit, the villagers divide into small groups to eat, whilst the young men who are to fight move away and separate into bands of friends. Centre stage is a roughly circular area about 200 metres in diameter and cordoned off by wire.

Within this sacred circle are three stone altars, the largest of which holds a cross, garlanded in flowers—an Aztec touch—and dedicated to the Catholic Santa Cruz. The fights themselves are preceded by a curious mixture of Spanish and Nahuatl chants and by mid-day, with the sun at the peak of its power, the fighting has begun. Having entered a human circle, the contestants crouch down on one knee and hold a 'jaguar tail' of rope in one hand whilst the remainder is loosely coiled around the waist. They swish their rope tails just as a real jaguar flips its tail from side to side when stalking its prey. A middleman convenes a fight and two contestants stand and 'paw' each other for a few minutes, making growling noises and doubtless testing their opponent's reflexes.

After this warming-up, they begin to fight in earnest. The ferocity of the fist

One of several holy altars within the sacred circle. Catholic Spanish and Aztec elements combine in the candles and flowers respectively. The womenfolk of Acatlán kneel, place candles at the base and chant hymns. *Photo, Author*

fights is all the more intriguing as both contestants belong to the same village and doubtless know each other well in everyday life. Fighters often completely knock out an opponent, who is then carried outside the wire circle before any attempts are made to revive him. The fights themselves are strictly governed, with only blows to the head and chest being allowed. If a contestant commits a foul, for example, by kicking or striking when an opponent is down, he risks losing the contest by default and, on occasion, being attacked by the onlookers. Two or three fights take place simultaneously, and blood is indeed spilt for the jaguar god. By mid-afternoon the fighting has subsided and the villagers make their way back down the mountainside.

Sunset the next day finds the villagers gathered around one of Acatlán's largest freshwater springs to see more traditional dancing and eat soup and *tamales*, both made from maize. On this occasion some of the younger boys dress as jaguars and imitate the more violent fighting of the previous day. A few weeks later the rains come, and the blood offerings to the jaguar deity are deemed to have been acceptable. The maize flourishes and the village is secure for another year.

Acatlán can indeed be called the village of the jaguar. Although much of the symbolism surrounding its unique jaguar fights can be traced back to Aztec times, between 1300 and 1519, its essential features go much further back into Mexico's prehistoric past. The area that is today the state of Guerrero was known to the Olmecs who, perhaps by trade or colonisation, acquired their precious greenstones of jade and serpentine in this volcanically active region. Just a few kilometres from Acatlán itself is the painted cave of Oxtotitlán, decorated with the remains of an elaborate mural depicting an Olmec ruler sitting on a jaguar throne. A few kilometres further on is the famous Olmec cave of Juxtlahuaca where, a mile or so inside, lie similarly dramatic murals depicting a standing Olmec figure dressed in a jaguar skin. Acatlán's springtime jaguar fights are thus a living testament to the tenacity of age-old beliefs.

The Sorcerer's Soul

Superstitions surrounding the jaguar also survive in other remote parts of Central America. Among the Maya Indians of Chamula in southern Mexico, humans are believed to possess animal soul-companions, different animals establishing personal links with certain individuals in an hierarchical fashion. Occupying the topmost level are animals associated with the rich and powerful—the most common of which is the jaguar. Shamans, religious leaders and local politicians—individuals who wield considerable influence—are all believed to have jaguar soul-companions.

In one particular instance a Chamula shaman, eager to display his power as a curer, tells how his jaguar soul killed strangers and in this way protected his family and his community. Real jaguars are seldom seen in the highland area of Chamula, and are associated with the tropical lowlands; this, combined with

Beliefs surrounding Acatlán's jaguar-fights start young. Here two village children look on at an associated gathering at the town's main water source on the day after the fights. *Photo, Author*

the fact that the jaguar is in any case seldom seen by virtue of being a nocturnal predator, makes it a powerful soul-companion to the inhabitants of Chamula.

Spanish missionary activity in the area has brought about an interesting adjunct. When Catholic priests first came to Chamula they introduced St Jerome, whose image was accompanied by a lion lying at his feet. In their turn the local inhabitants interpreted this feline as a jaguar, and St Jerome as the powerful protector of animal souls. Today this European saint is a curious mixture of Catholic sainthood and Pre-Columbian deity, referred to as St Jerome, Our Father Jaguar.

The Living Spirit

Beliefs surrounding the jaguar are still acknowledged in many parts of the Americas, their importance and symbolism alive after the passage of untold centuries. For ancient peoples jaguars symbolised the power and control which humans believed they could exercise over the ambivalent forces of nature. The fact that real jaguars are the most successful of America's carnivores was the starting point from which a whole set of cultural beliefs and ideas were elaborated, equating with the jaguar men of pre-eminent social, political and mystical status. As the jaguar was lord of the jungle and master of its animals, so priests and kings were lords of their societies and masters of men.

As civilisations became larger and more sophisticated, so the religious beliefs and political mechanisms which characterised them became more complex. However, the distinctively Amerindian world-view did not disappear—it was not replaced by newer creeds or alternative cosmic views. It simply became more elaborate. The jaguar, so important to hunting and gathering societies, took on a more sophisticated look, and notions of power and success were used to lend legitimacy to royal dynasties, full-time priesthoods and military orders. The jaguar icon now found itself translated into the more permanent and impressive media of stone sculpture, gold, pottery figurines and brightly coloured mural paintings and textiles.

It is perhaps no coincidence that Mexico's first civilisation, the Olmec, and Andean Peru's precocious Chavín culture, both flourishing in the period between 1200 and 400 BC, display the symbol of the jaguar in their graphic and impressive official art styles. Prowess, supernatural power and political success are intricately woven into a rich tapestry of beliefs and attitudes which reflect in part the ideologies of these prehistoric civilisations.

Universal human concerns, expressed through feline imagery, were amongst some of the most distinctive Amerindian ways in which ancient civilisations blended the real and the imaginary. In a world alive with dangerous spirits, humans 'became jaguars' in order to survive and dominate the natural and social worlds. The jaguar was the vehicle for expressing the belief that the uncertainties of life and death could be controlled. The spirit of the jaguar, ever-present and ever-threatening, embodied the soul of Pre-Columbian America.

BIBLIOGRAPHY

CHAPTER 1: A NEW WORLD

BANKES, G. *Peru before Pizarro*. Phaidon, Oxford, 1977.

BRAY, W. *Everyday Life of the Aztecs*. Batsford, London, 1968.

COE, M. *Mexico*. Thames & Hudson, London, 1984 (revised ed).

COE, M. *The Maya*. Thames & Hudson, London, 1987 (revised ed).

DAVIES, N. *The Aztecs*. Macmillan, London, 1973.

FAGAN, B. M. *The Greeat Journey*. Thames & Hudson, London, 1987.

KENDALL, A. *Everyday Life of the Incas*. Batsford, London, 1973.

LUMBRERAS, L. G. *The Peoples and Cultures of Ancient Peru*. Smithsonian Institution Press, Washington, 1974.

PARRY, J. H. *The Discovery of South America*. Paul Elek, London, 1979.

PORTER WEAVER, M. *The Aztecs, Maya and their Predecessors*. Academic Press, New York and London, 1981 (second ed).

SAUER, C. O. *The Early Spanish Main*. University of California Press, Berkeley and Los Angeles, 1969.

CHAPTER 2: THE OLMEC DISCOVERY

BEYER, H. 'Bibliografía [Frans Blom y Oliver La Farge] Tribes and Temples'. *El México Antiguo*, vol 2, nos 11–12, pp 305–13. Mexico.

BLOM, F. and LA FARGE, O. *Tribes and Temples*, 2 vols. Tulane University Press, New Orleans, 1926–7.

COE, M. *America's First Civilisation: Discovering the Olmec*. American Heritage, New York, 1968.

COVARRUBIAS, M. *Mexico South: The Isthmus of Tehuantepec*. Alfred Knopf, New York, 1946.

MELGAR, J. M. 'Antiguedes mexicanas, notable escultura antigua'. *Boletín de la Sociedad Mexicana de Geografía y Estadística*, época 2, vol 3. pp 104–9. Mexico.

SAVILLE, M. H. 'Votive Axes from Ancient Mexico, parts 1 & 2'. *Indian Notes*, vol 6, pp 266–99 and 335–42. Museum of the American Indian, Heye Foundation, New York.

STEPHENS, J. L. *Incidents of Travel in Central America, Chiapas and Yucatan*, 2 vols, ed. V. W. Von Hagen. University of Oklahoma Press, Norman, 1962.

STIRLING, M. 'Expedition Unearths Buried Masterpieces of Carved Jade'. *National Geographic*, vol 80, pp 277–302, Washington, 1941.

STIRLING, M. 'La Venta's Green Stone Tigers'. *National Geographic*, vol 84, pp 321–32, Washington, 1943.

STIRLING, M. 'Stone Monuments of Southern Mexico'. *Bureau of American Ethnology, Bulletin 138*, Washington, 1943.

STIRLING, M. 'On the Trail of La Venta Man'. *National Geographic*, vol 91, pp 137–72, Washington, 1947.

STIRLING, M. 'Stone Monuments of the Río Chiquito, Veracruz, Mexico'. *Bureau of American Ethnology, Bulletin 157*, pp 1–24, Washington, 1955.

STIRLING, M. 'Early History of the Olmec Problem', in *Dumbarton Oaks Conference on the Olmec*, ed. E. P. Benson, pp 1–8, Dumbarton Oaks, Washington, 1968.

CHAPTER 3: RECOVERING THE OLMEC CIVILISATION

BENSON, E. P. (ed). *Conference on the Olmec*. Dumbarton Oaks, Washington, 1968.

BERNAL, I. *The Olmec World*. University of California Press, Berkeley and Los Angeles, 1969.

COE, M. *The Jaguar's Children: Pre-Classic Central Mexico*. Museum of Primitive Art, New York, 1965.

COE, M. 'San Lorenzo and the Olmec Civilisation', in *Dumbarton Oaks Conference on the Olmec*. ed. E. P. Benson, pp 41–78. Dumbarton Oaks, Washington, 1968.

COE, M. and DIEHL, R. *In the Land of the Olmec*, 2 vols. Univesity of Texas Press, Austin, Texas and London, 1980.

DRUCKER, P. 'La Venta Tabasco: A Study of Olmec Ceramics and Art'. *Bureau of American Ethnology, Bulletin 153*. Washington, 1952.

DRUCKER, P., HEIZER, R. and SQUIER, R. 'Excavations at La Venta, Tabasco, 1955'. *Bureau of American Ethnology, Bulletin 170*. Washington, 1959.

GROVE, D. *The Olmec Paintings of Oxtotitlán Cave, Guerrero, Mexico*. Studies in Pre-Columbian Art and Archaeology no 6. Dumbarton Oaks, Washington, 1970.

GROVE, D. *Chalcatzingo*. Thames & Hudson, London, 1984.

SOUSTELLE, J. *Les Olmeques*. Les Éditions Arthaud, Paris, 1979.

CHAPTER 4: OLMEC ART, SOCIETY AND RELIGION

BENSON, E. P. (ed). *Conference on the Olmec*. Dumbarton Oaks, Washington, 1968.

BENSON, E. P. (ed). *The Cult of the Feline*. Dumbarton Oaks, Washington, 1972.

BENSON, E. P. (ed). *The Olmec and their Neighbours*. Dumbarton Oaks, Washington, 1981.

BERNAL, I. *The Olmec World*. University of California Press, Berkeley and Los Angeles, 1969.

COE, M. 'The Olmec Style and its Distributions', in *Handbook of Middle American Indians*, vol 3, part 2, pp 739–75. University of Texas Press, Austin, 1965.

COE, M. 'Olmec Jaguars and Olmec Kings', in *The Cult of the Feline*, ed. E. P. Benson, pp 1–12. Dumbarton Oaks, Washington, 1972.

COE, M. and DIEHL, R. *In the Land of the Olmec*, 2 vols. University of Texas Press, Austin, Texas and London, 1980.

FLANNERY, K. 'The Olmec and the Valley of Oaxaca', in *Dumbarton Oaks Conference on the Olmec*, ed. E. P. Benson, pp 79–118. Dumbarton Oaks, Washington, 1968.

FURST, P. T. 'The Olmec Were-Jaguar Motif in the Light of Ethnographic Reality', in *Dumbarton Oaks Conference on the Olmec*, ed. E. P. Benson, pp 143–74. Dumbarton Oaks, Washington, 1968.

GROVE, D. *The Olmec Paintings of Oxtotitlán Cave, Guerrero, Mexico*. Studies in Pre-Columbian Art and Archaeology no 6. Dumbarton Oaks, Washington, 1970.

JORALEMON, P. D. *A Study of Olmec Iconography*. Studies in Pre-Columbian Art and Archaeology no 7. Dumbarton Oaks, Washington, 1971.

STIRLING, M. 'The Olmec, Artists in Jade', in *Essays in Pre-Columbian Art and Archaeology*, ed. S. K. Lothrop, pp 42–59. Harvard University Press, Cambridge, Massachusetts, 1964.

CHAPTER 5: THE DISCOVERY AND ARCHAEOLOGY OF THE CHAVÍN CIVILISATION

BENSON, E. P. (ed). *Dumbarton Oaks Conference on Chavín*. Dumbarton Oaks, Washington, 1971.

BURGER, R. L. 'The Radiocarbon Evidence for the Temporal Priority of Chavín de Huántar'. *American Antiquity*, vol 46, pp 592–602. Salt Lake City, 1981.

BURGER, R. L. 'Pojoc and Waman Wain: Two Early Horizon villages in the Chavín Heartland'. *Ñawpa Pacha*, vol 20, pp 3–40. Berkeley, 1983.

BURGER, R. L. *The Prehistoric Occupation of Chavín de Huántar, Peru*. University of California Publications in Anthropology vol 14. University of California Press, Berkeley, Los Angeles and London, 1984.

CARRIÓN CACHOT, R. 'La Cultura Chavín; dos Nuevas Colonias: Kuntur Wasi y Ancón'. *Revista del Museo Nacional de Antropología y Arqueología*, vol II, no 1, pp 99–172. Lima, 1948.

IZUMI, S. 'The Development of the Formative Culture in the Ceja de Montaña: A Viewpoint Based on the Materials from the Kotosh Site', in *Dumbarton Oaks Conference on Chavín*, ed. E. P. Benson, pp 49–72. Dumbarton Oaks, Washington, 1971.

KANO, O. *The Origins of the Chavín Culture*. Studies in Pre-Columbian Art and Archaeology no 22. Dumbarton Oaks, Washington, 1979.

LARCO HOYLE, R. *Los Cupisniques*. Casa Editora La Crónica y Variedades, Lima, 1941.

LATHRAP, D. W. *The Upper Amazon*. Thames & Hudson, London, 1970.

LATHRAP, D. W. 'The Tropical Forest and the Cultural Context of Chavín', in

Dumbarton Oaks Conference on Chavín, ed. E. P. Benson, pp 73–100. Dumbarton Oaks, Washington, 1971.

LOTHROP, S. K. 'Gold Ornaments of Chavín Style from Chongoyape, Peru'. *American Antiquity*, vol VI, no 3, pp 250–62, 1941.

LUMBRERAS, L. G. 'Excavaciones en el templo antiguo de Chavín (sector R): informe de la sexta compaña'. *Ñawpa Pacha*, vol 15, pp 1–38, 1977.

LUMBRERAS, L. G. and OLAZABAL, H. A. 'Informe preliminar sobre las galerias interiores de Chavín (primera temporada de trabajos)'. *Revista del Museo Nacional*, vol 34 (1965–66); pp 143–97, Lima, 1969.

TELLO, J. C. 'Wira Kocha'. *Inca*, vol 1, no 1, pp 93–320, enero-marzo, 1923; no 3, pp 583–606, julio-septiembre, 1923, Lima.

TELLO, J. C. 'Discovery of the Chavín Culture in Peru'. *American Antiquity*, vol IX, no 1, pp 135–60. Menasha, 1943.

TELLO, J. C. *Chavín: Cultura Matriz de la Civilización Andina*. Primera Parte. Publicación Antropología del Archivo 'Julio C Tello' de la Universidad Nacional Mayor de San Marcos, Lima, 1960.

WILLEY, G. R. 'The Chavín Problem: A Review and Critique'. *Southwestern Journal of Anthropology*, vol 7, no 2, pp 103–44, Albuquerque.

CHAPTER 6: CHAVÍN ART, RELIGION AND SOCIETY

AYRES, E. D. 'Rubbings from Chavín de Huántar, Peru'. *American Antiquity*, vol 27, no 2, pp 238–45, 1961.

BENSON, E. P. (ed). *Dumbarton Oaks Conference on Chavín*. Dumbarton Oaks, Washington, 1971.

BENSON, E. P. (ed). *The Cult of the Feline*. Dumbarton Oaks, Washington, 1972.

CARRIÓN CACHOT, R. 'La Cultura Chavín; dos Nuevas Colonias: Kuntur Wasi y Ancón'. *Revista del Museo Nacional de Antropología y Arquelogía*, vol II, no 1, pp 99–172. Lima.

CONKLIN, W. J. 'The Revolutionary Weaving Inventions of the Early Horizon'. *Ñawpa Pacha*, vol 16, pp 1–12, Berkeley, 1978.

CORDY-COLLINS, A. 'Chavín Art: Its Shamanic/Hallucinogenic Origins', in *Pre-Columbian Art History: Selected Readings*, eds A. Cordy-Collins and J. Stern, pp 353–62. Costello Educational, Tunbridge Wells, 1980.

CORDY-COLLINS, A. 'Cotton and the Staff God: Analysis of an Ancient Chavín Textile', in *The Junius B. Bird Pre-Columbian Textile Conference*, ed. A. P. Rowe, E. P. Benson and A.-L. Schaffer, pp 51–60, Dumbarton Oaks, Washington, 1979.

DWYER, J. P. and DWYER, E. D. 'The Paracas Cemeteries: Mortuary Patterns in a Peruvian South Coastal Tradition', in *Death and the Afterlife in Pre-Columbian America*, ed. E. P. Benson, pp 105–28. Dumbarton Oaks, Washington, 1975.

LATHRAP, D. W. *The Upper Amazon*. Thames & Hudson, London, 1970.

LATHRAP, D. W. 'Gifts of the Cayman: Some Thoughts on the Subsistence Basis of Chavín', in *Variations in Anthropology*, eds. D. W. Lathrap and Douglas. Illinois Archaeological Survey, pp 91—105, Urbana, 1973.

LOTHROP, S. K. 'Gold Ornaments of Chavín Style from Chongoyape, Peru'. *American Antiquity*, vol VI, no 3, pp 250–62, Menasha, 1941.

LUMBRERAS, L. G. 'Towards a Re-evaluation of Chavín', in *Dumbarton Oaks Conference on Chavín*, ed. E. P. Benson, pp 1–28. Dumbarton Oaks, Washington, 1971.

LUMBRERAS, L. G. 'Excavaciones en el templo antiguo de Chavín (sector R): informe de la sexta compaña'. *Ñawpa Pacha*, vol 15, pp 1–38, Berkeley, 1977.

ROE, P. G. *A Further Exploration of the Rowe Chavín Seriation and its Implications for North Central Coast Chronology*. Dumbarton Oaks, Washington, 1974.

ROE, P.G. 'Recent discoveries in Chavín art: some speculations on methodology and significance in the analysis of a figural style', in *El Dorado*, vol 3, no 1, pp 1–41, 1978.

ROWE, J. H. 'Form and Meaning in Chavín Art', in *Peruvian Archaeology: Selected Readings*, ed J. H. Rowe and D. Menzel, pp 72–103. Peek Publications, Palo Alto, 1967.

SHARON, D. *Wizard of the Four Winds*. The Free Press, New York and London, 1978.

TELLO, J. C. 'Wira Kocha'. *Inca*, vol 1, no 1, pp 93–320, enero-marzo, 1923; no 3, pp 583–606, julio-septiembre, 1923, Lima.

TELLO, J. C. *Chavín: Cultura Matriz de la Civilización Andina*. Primera Parte. Publicación Antropología del Archivo 'Julio C Tello' de la Universidad Nacional Mayor de San Marcos, Lima, 1960.

WILLEY, G. R. 'The Early Great Art Styles and the Rise of the Pre-Columbian Civilisations'. *American Antiquity*, vol 64, no 1, pp 1–14. Menasha, 1962.

CHAPTER 7: SHAMANS IN THE RAINFOREST

BUTT-COLSON, A. 'The Shaman's Legal Role', in *Revista do Museu Paulista*, NS XVI, 1965–6, pp 151–86. São Paulo.

BUTT-COLSON, A. 'The Akawaio Shaman', in *Carib-Speaking Indians: Culture, Society and Language*, ed. E. Basso, pp 43–65. University of Arizona Press, Tucson, 1977.

DOLE, G. 'Shamanism and Political Control among the Kuikuru', in *Peoples and Cultures of Native South America*, ed. D. Gross, pp 294–311, New York, 1973.

ELIADE, M. *Shamanism: Archaic Techniques of Ecstasy*. Bollingen Series LXXVI, Pantheon Books, New York, 1964.

GOLDMAN, I. *The Cubeo*. University of Illinois Press, Urbana, Chicago and London, 1979 (second ed).

HALIFAX, J. *Shamanic Voices*. Penguin Books, Harmondsworth, 1979.

HARNER *The Jívaro*. Natural History Press, New York, 1972.

HUGH-JONES, S. *The Palm and the Pleiades*. Cambridge University Press, 1979.

KENSINGER, K. M. 'Cashinahua Medicine and Medicine Men', in *Native South Americans*, ed P. J. Lyon, pp 283–88. Little, Brown, Boston, 1974.

LA BARRE, W. *The Ghost Dance*. Allen & Unwin, London, 1970.

LEWIS, I. M. *Ecstatic Religion: An Anthropological Study of Spirit Possession and Shamanism*. Penguin Books, Harmondsworth, 1975.

Reichel-Dolmatoff, G. *Amazonian Cosmos.* University of Chicago Press, 1971.
Shirokogoroff, S. M. *Psychomental Complex of the Tungus.* London, 1935.
Silverman, J. 'Shamans and Acute Schizophrenia'. *American Anthropologist*, vol 69, pp 21–32, 1967.
Van Gennep, A. *The Rites of Passage.* Routledge & Kegan Paul, London, 1977.

CHAPTER 8: SHAMANS AND JAGUARS

Anderson, E. F. *Peyote the Divine Cactus.* University of Arizona Press, Tucson, 1980.
Furst, P. T. (ed). *Flesh of the Gods.* Praeger, New York, 1972.
Harner, M. J. *The Jívaro.* Natural History Press, New York, 1972.
Harner, M. J. *Hallucinogens and Shamanism.* Oxford University Press, 1973.
Mortimer, W. G. *History of Coca 'The Divine Plant of the Incas'.* And/Or Press, San Francisco, 1974.
Reichel-Dolmatoff, G. *Amazonian Cosmos.* University of Chicago Press, 1971.
Reichel-Dolmatoff, G. *The Shaman and the Jaguar.* Temple University Press, Philadelphia, 1975.
Schultes, R. and Hofmann, A. *Plants of the Gods.* Hutchinson, London, 1980.
Urton, G. (ed). *Animal Myths and Metaphors in South America.* University of Utah Press, Salt Lake City, 1985.
Wassén, S. H. 'On Concepts of Disease among Amerindian Tribal Groups'. *Journal of Ethnopharmacology*, vol 3, pp 285–94. 1979.
Wasson, R. G. 'The Hallucinogenic Mushrooms of Mexico'. *Transactions of the New York Academy of Sciences.* Series II, vol 21, no 4, pp 325–39. New York.
Wasson, R. G. 'Ololiuhqui and other hallucinogens of Mexico', in *Summa anthropologica en homenaje a Roberto J. Weitlaner*, pp 329–48. Mexico.
Wasson, R. G. *Maria Sabina and her Mazatec Mushroom Velada.* Harcourt, Brace Jovanovich, New York.

CHAPTER 9: SYMBOL OF ROYALTY AND SACRIFICE

Benson, E. P. *The Mochica.* Thames & Hudson, London, 1972.
Benson, E. P. (ed). *The Cult of the Feline.* Dumbarton Oaks, Washington, 1972.
Benson, E. P. *A Man and a Feline in Mochica Art.* Studies in Pre-Columbian Art and Archaeology no 14, Dumbarton Oaks, Washington, 1974.
Benson, E. P. 'The Classic Maya Use of Jaguar Accessories', in *Fourth Palenque Round Table*, Vol Vi, ed. E. P. Benson. San Francisco, 1985.
Cordy-Collins, A. 'Cotton and the Staff God: Analysis of an Ancient Chavín Textile', in *The Junius B. Bird Pre-Columbian Textile Conference*, ed. A. P. Rowe, E. P. Benson and A.-L. Schaffer, pp 51–60. Dumbarton Oaks, Washington, 1979.
Davies, N. *The Aztecs.* Macmillan, London, 1973.
Diehl, R. *Tula.* Thames & Hudson, London, 1983.
Duran, F. D. *Book of the Gods and Rites and The Ancient Calendar.* University of Oklahoma Press, Norman, 1971.
Henderson, J. S. *The World of the Ancient Maya.* Orbis, London, 1981.

MARCUS, J. *Emblem and State in the Classic Maya Lowlands*. Dumbarton Oaks, Washington, 1976.

PASZTORY, E. *Aztec Art*. Abrams, New York, 1983.

ROBICSEK, F. 'Mats and Jaguars', in *A Study in Maya Art and History: The Mat Symbol*, ed. F. Robicsek, pp 108–18. The Museum of the American Indian, Heye Foundation, New York, 1975.

ROBICSEK, F. and HALES, D. 'Maya Heart Sacrifice: Cultural Perspective and Surgical Technique', in *Ritual Human Sacrifice in Mesoamerica*, ed. E. H. Boone, pp 49–90. Dumbarton Oaks, Washington, 1984.

SAUNDERS, N. J. 'Tezcatlipoca: Jaguar Metaphors of an Aztec Deity'. Paper delivered to the 46th International Congress of Americanists, Amsterdam, 1988.

SAWYER, A. R. 'Paracas and Nazca Iconography', in *Essays in Pre-Columbian Art and Archaeology*, ed. S. K. Lothrop, pp 269–98. Harvard University Press, 1961.

SAWYER, A. R. 'The Feline in Paracas Art', in *Cult of the Feline*, ed. E. P. Benson, pp 91–115. Dumbarton Oaks, Washington, 1972.

SELER, E. *Gesammelte Abhandlungen zur amerikanischen Sprach- und Altertumskunde*, 5 vols, Berlin, 1902–23.

THOMPSON, J. E. S. *The Rise and Fall of Maya Civilisation*. University of Oklahoma Press, Norman, 1966.

THOMPSON, J. E. S. *Maya History and Religion*. University of Oklahoma Press, Norman, 1970.

ZUIDEMA, R. T. 'The Lion in the City: Royal Symbols of Transition in Cuzco'. *Journal of Latin American Lore*, vol 9, no 1, pp 39–100, 1983.

CHAPTER 10: THE ENDURING BELIEF

CORDRY, D. *Mexican Masks*. University of Texas Press. Austin and London, 1980.

ECKHOLM, G. F. 'The Archaeological Significance of Mirrors in the New World'. *Atti del XL Congresso Internazionale degli Americanisti*, vol 1, pp 133–35. Rome and Genoa, 1972.

GOSSEN, G. H. 'Animal souls and human destiny in Chamula'. *MAN*, vol 10, no 3, pp 448–61, 1975.

PERRY, R. *The World of the Jaguar*. David & Charles, 1970.

RABINOWITZ, A. *Jaguar*. Collins, London, 1987.

SAUNDERS, N. J. 'The Day of the Jaguar: Rainmaking in a Mexican Village'. *Geographical Magazine*, vol LV, pp 398–405, London, August 1983.

SAUNDERS, N. J. 'Jaguars, Rain and Blood; Religious Symbolism in Acatlán, Guerrero, Mexico'. *Cambridge Anthropology*, vol 9, no 1, pp 77–81, Cambridge, 1984.

SAUNDERS, N. J. 'Chatoyer: Anthropological Reflections on Archaeological Mirrors', in N. J. Saunders and O. de Montmollin (eds.), *Recent Studies in Pre-Columbian Archaeology*, BAR International Series 421, Oxford, 1988.

WILLIAMS-GARCIA, R. *Fiestas de La Santa Cruz en Zitlala*. Fonadan, Mexico City.

INDEX

INDEX

175